CHARLESTON
in the Age of the Pinckneys

CHARLESTON
in the Age of the Pinckneys

BY GEORGE C. ROGERS, JR.

UNIVERSITY OF SOUTH CAROLINA PRESS

To Jay and Ann

Preface to the Paperback Edition

DURING THE LAST TWO YEARS many persons have asked me to secure a reprinting of this little book on Charleston. The University of Oklahoma Press first printed *Charleston in the Age of the Pinckneys* in 1969 in their Centers of Civilization Series. Now the University of South Carolina Press has decided to add this title to its growing list of Charlestoniana. I am most grateful therefore to have this opportunity to make a few minor corrections in spelling, style, and identification as well as to remove several typographical errors. Although the reviewers were generous in their praise, many regretted that the volume contained no maps. We have thus inserted two maps and at the same time have added a number of illustrations.

I have felt no need to alter the text or to change my interpretation. Indeed I have been urged to leave my original statement as it is. There are, however, a number of books, published in the last decade, which provide additional insights into the lives of the members of the Pinckney family and into the history of the city and of the state. *The Letterbook of Eliza Lucas Pinckney, 1739–1763*, carefully edited by Elise Pinckney, appeared in 1972. The most complete study of the Pinckney family is that provided by Frances Leigh Williams in *A Founding Family: The Pinckneys of South Carolina* (1978).

Lewis P. Jones's *South Carolina: A Synoptic History for Laymen* (1971) is the most readable history of the state. Peter Wood with his publication of *Black Majority* in 1974 has changed our views of the role of blacks in early South Carolina. Steven A. Channing's *Crisis of Fear: Secession in South Carolina* (1970) and E. Milby Burton's *The Siege of Charleston, 1861–1865* (1970) provide provocative statements and fresh overviews for the late antebellum and Civil War periods.

The South Carolina Tricentennial Commission (1967–1971) sponsored a number of important works. Among the Tricentennial Editions are *Jacob Eckhard's Choirmaster's Book of 1809* with an introduction by George W. Williams (1971), the edition by Walter B. Edgar of *The Letterbook of Robert Pringle, 1737–1745* (1972), and *The Letters of Freeman, Etc.* edited by Robert M. Weir (1977). Among the Tricentennial Studies are Converse D. Clowse's *Economic Beginnings in Colonial South Carolina, 1670–1730* (1971), George Smith McCowen's *The British Occupation of Charleston, 1780–82* (1972), and Carl J. Vipperman's *The Rise of Rawlins Lowndes, 1721–1800* (1978). Among the Tricentennial Booklets are Robert M. Weir's *"A Most Important Epocha": The Coming of the Revolution in South Carolina* (1970) and Russell F. Weigley's *The Partisan War: The South Carolina Campaign of 1780–1782* (1970).

Clarence L. Ver Steeg in *Origins of a Southern Mosaic* (1975) has fitted the South Carolina story into that of the southeast in general and Phinizy Spalding in *Oglethorpe in America* (1977) continues to throw light on South Carolina history by telling us what was happening in Georgia.

The Papers of Henry Laurens, edited by the late Philip M. Hamer, George C. Rogers, Jr., and David R. Chesnutt, has in eight volumes (1747–1773) given the day-by-day detail of life in the commercial, social, and political world of Charleston.

I still cherish this little volume as my own favorite book among those I have written. I am willing to present it once again as an introduction to the larger stories of the state.

Acknowledgments

THE AUTHOR WISHES TO THANK Professors Robert M. Weir and Frank Durham of the University of South Carolina for their criticisms of this manuscript and the members of the Quill Club of Columbia, South Carolina, for patiently listening while portions of several chapters were read to them. Mrs. Evelyn Frazier made helpful suggestions with reference to style. Miss Anna Rutledge has on many occasions brought to the author's attention little-known but interesting facets of South Carolina's history.

Without the continuing help of Mrs. Mary Elizabeth Prior, E. I. Inabinett, and Charles Lee and the staffs of their respective institutions, the South Carolina Historical Society, the South Caroliniana Library of the University of South Carolina, and the South Carolina Department of Archives and History, the writing of South Carolina history could not proceed. Mrs. Davy-Jo S. Ridge and her staff in the Reference Room of the McKissick Library of the University of South Carolina have willingly answered many queries. Miss Helen McCormack has selected the line drawing used on page 67.

Professor Robert D. Ochs, head of the Department of History in the University of South Carolina, has constantly smoothed the way so that the writing of this manuscript has been made easier. The author is also most grateful to the Research Committee of the University of South Carolina for providing funds for typing and to Mrs. Esther

Markel and Mrs. Nina F. Brooks who patiently typed and retyped this manuscript.

Columbia, South Carolina
January 12, 1969

GEORGE C. ROGERS, JR.

Prologue

ON THE EVENING of June 11, 1766, the ship *Fonthill*, direct from London, arrived off Charleston bar. On board was George III's newly appointed royal governor for the province of South Carolina—the Right Honorable Lord Charles Greville Montagu, second son of the Duke of Manchester. Before him lay the young city of Charleston. To some it was a self-conscious seat of empire, the greatest port between Philadelphia and the West Indies, the center of a vast web of commerce that spiraled out across the Atlantic and fanned back as far as the Tennessee and Mississippi rivers. To Lord Montagu, it was his capital. When the signal guns of Fort Johnson boomed out a welcome, Charleston made ready to receive him with ceremonies befitting his rank and her position.

Early the next morning rejoicing over sea and land greeted the new governor. Before him lay all the ships in the harbor with their pendants unfurled against the sky. Then from across the gray waters of the Ashley and Cooper rivers drifted the sweet pealing of the bells atop St. Michael's. As the *Fonthill* swept across the waves toward the city, the booming of cannon announced her route. From Fort Johnson came a fifteen-gun salute, followed by another from Broughton's Battery on Oyster Point, and ending with the guns of Craven's Bastion at the northern end of the well-fortified city.

No sooner had the *Fonthill* dropped anchor than the clerk of the Council and the master in chancery went aboard. It was their duty to convey the compliments of

Lieutenant-Governor William Bull II and to arrange for the order of public events scheduled in honor of the new governor. The Governor, resplendent in his official robes, accompanied by these officials, left the ship via barge for shore. As they approached the wharf, Captain Christopher Gadsden's Artillery Company, composed of sixty sons of the well-to-do, uniformed in blue breeches, crimson jackets, and gold-laced hats, fired the guns of Granville's Bastion at the southern end of the city.

On land Lord Charles was met by the Honorable Thomas Skottowe and the Honorable John Burn, the junior members of the Council, who extended the congratulations of that body on his safe arrival. Between two lines of brilliantly dressed Charleston Regiment of Foot, the Governor's suite was conducted along Broad Street to the Council chamber in the new State House, where the Governor was introduced to the Lieutenant-Governor and to the other members of the Council. The Governor's royal commission appointing him captain-general, governor, and commander-in-chief, and vice-admiral of the royal province of South Carolina was read. Then his Lordship, with his retinue, proceeded east on Broad Street and south along the Bay to Granville's Bastion. The officers of the crown and the gentlemen of distinction were preceded by the deputy provost marshal, Roger Pinckney, who, with the sword of state held high before him, led them through the two lines of the Regiment of Foot, which were now extended down to Granville's Bastion. Here the royal commission, as was the custom, was read to the people by the clerk of the Council. No sooner had the last words died away than three loud huzzas went up from the crowd for their new governor. The cheers were quickly followed by a round of firing from the bastion's guns and a volley from the regiment. As the procession returned to the chamber, the new governor was greeted along the way by the "loud and hearty acclamation" of the people. Here Lord Charles qualified for the governor's office by swearing an oath of allegiance to the crown, an oath to support the Protestant succession against all Popish recusants, and an oath to carry out the laws of the province.

Afterward he was conducted into the June air, and again by foot parade he proceeded to Dillon's Tavern for an elegant dinner, one which was attended by the leading citizens and the civil and military officers.

While the elite dined, the city and harbor blazed with illuminations hanging from the city's balconies and stringing from the ship's masts. The inhabitants at Haddrell's Point across the Cooper River and at James Island across the Ashley were also not reticent in their demonstrations of joy. Here and there, not unknown to the new governor, bonfires burned across the harbor waters.

Lord Charles Montagu's welcome was no different from that accorded all royal governors by the loyal people of South Carolina. So welcomed had been Robert Johnson on December 15, 1730; James Glen on December 17, 1743; William Henry Lyttelton on June 1, 1756; and Thomas Boone on December 22, 1761. Only Lord William Campbell, arriving on June 18, 1775, was received in "sullen silence." By that time the American Revolution had begun.

Contents

Note: The maps and illustrations will be found
following page 88.

CHARLESTON
in the Age of the Pinckneys

I.

The Economic Base

CHARLESTON WAS A CENTER of the British empire because she was a crossroads of trade. Her golden age of commerce lasted one hundred years—from the 1730's to the 1820's. During the 1730's Charleston was booming amid a great economic expansion; during the 1820's she was in full decline as an economic depression spread over the state. The 1730's coincided with the first decade of royal rule and the establishment of a strong provincial government; the 1820's, with the movement that culminated in nullification. The rise, flourishing, and decline of Charleston's greatness all took place between these two eras.

Two famous prints of Charleston, of 1739 and 1774, show the harbor filled with sailing vessels. During the winter months from November to March there were often one hundred vessels riding at anchor in the harbor. The *Gazette* of January 5, 1767, noted only eighty-five but commented that they were "fewer than usual." During the year two hundred to three hundred topsail vessels would clear the port. Vessels of all kinds, ships, brigantines, snows, schooners, and sloops, came after the hurricane season in order to transport the crops to market. Captured xebecs and guarda-costas, Indian pettiaugers and canoes, as well as plantation flats, added to the traffic.

Charleston's golden age coincided with the last century of the age of sailing vessels. As long as the age of sail lasted, Charleston was on the main Atlantic highway, which circumnavigated the Bermuda High. Vessels leaving England, or leaving any European port for North America, generally sailed southwestwardly to the Azores to catch the trade winds and then with full sail made for the West Indies, Barbados standing out front like a doorman to welcome all to the New World. They next made their way through the West Indies to the Gulf Stream. From the Florida Keys to Cape Hatteras they hugged the American coast before veering off to England and northern Europe. It was a great circle, and Charleston was on its western edge. The first settlers on the *Carolina, Albemarle,* and *Port Royal* in 1669-70 had followed this route via Barbados, Nevis, Bahamas, and Bermuda to Carolina. Although the *Albemarle* was wrecked in the West Indies and the *Port Royal* in the Bahamas, the settlers reached Charleston.

In the 1760's, when the British Post Office established a regular trans-Atlantic postal system, the swift packets left Falmouth for Barbados, skirted the Leeward Islands to Jamaica, and made port at Pensacola, St. Augustine, and Charleston before returning home. Five vessels, the *Duncannon, Anna Theresa, Grantham, Grenville,* and *Hillsborough,* were on a regular schedule by 1766, each making annually two complete voyages around this circuit. The swiftest time on the leg from Charleston to Falmouth was twenty days. Even the Spanish galleons carrying the wealth of Peru and Mexico joined this great circle as they emerged from the Florida Straits. In June, 1766, six Spanish galleons were sighted off the South Carolina coast, just before they turned eastward for Spain.

These sailing vessels brought men from all parts of the Atlantic world to Charleston. From the British West Indies had come many of the original settlers: the Middletons and Schenkinghs from Barbados, the Lowndes and Rawlins from St. Kitts, the Lucases and Perrys from Antigua, the

4

Meylers and Whaleys from Jamaica, and the La Mottes from Grenada. The New England ship captains who peddled their goods in the southern colonies and in the West Indies often settled permanently in Charleston. Benjamin Smith's ancestor had come that way, as did Nathaniel Russell. The Darrells, Dickinsons, and Savages of Bermuda, who sought freight in all the British ports for their swift sloops, finally moved to the continental port. The largest group, of course, were English: Benjamin Stead from London, Samuel Brailsford from Bristol, William Price from Liverpool, George Austin from Shropshire, and Robert Raper from Yorkshire.

From the Continent had come the French Huguenots as early as the 1680's. The Manigaults and the Legarés had come by way of England to the Santee and then to Charleston; the Laurens by way of New York. Another great commercial people, the Dutch, were represented in Charleston by the Vander Horsts (who had accompanied William III to England), Alexander Vander Dussen, and Jacob Valk. The Sephardic Jews from the Iberian Peninsula were numerous enough in Charleston in 1750 to form a congregation. Moses Cohen, Isaac Da Costa, and Joseph Tobias, their leaders, had apparently come by way of London or Amsterdam. Aaron and Moses Lopez, who later joined this "Portuguese Jewish Congregation," arrived from Newport, Rhode Island.

After the union of England and Scotland in 1707, the Scots poured into Charleston, eventually contributing the largest numbers to the commercial community: George Seaman, John and David Deas, the Lennox brothers, the Michies, the Moultries, the Nesbits, the Johnstons, John Cleland, James Kinloch, Robert Pringle, and John Bowman. George Gabriel Powell, the Welshman, was born on the island of St. Helena, where his father had been governor. Andrew Rutledge arrived from Ireland.

In the eighteenth century many immigrants passed through Charleston on the way to the frontier. Ethnic societies were formed in the city by those who had already arrived and made a success and who then wanted to help their less fortunate, newly arriving compatriots. The St. Andrew's Society was formed in 1729, the St. George's Society in 1733, the South Carolina Society (mainly by French Protestants) in 1737, the German Friendly Society in 1766, the Friendly Sons of St. Patrick in 1774, the Hebrew Orphan Society in 1791, and the Hibernian Society in 1801, the last taking the place of the Friendly Sons of St. Patrick, which had disappeared. The primary object of all these societies was to aid distressed immigrants and to provide an education for orphans whose parents had died along the way. After a century, when the immigrant tide had subsided to a trickle, these societies became social clubs for descendants of charter members.

Pre-Revolutionary Charleston was a great receiving center, welcoming all who were enterprising. The Assembly, in order to strengthen the colony against internal tumult from the slaves and external danger from the Indians and the Spaniards, had instituted a township scheme to lure white Protestant settlers to Carolina. The "Palatine ships," as Henry Laurens called them, brought great numbers in the 1740's and early 1750's. These poor Protestants were provided with bounties, tools, and provisions. The Swiss who went to Purrysburg on the Savannah, the Germans who went to New Windsor on the Savannah, Orangeburg on the Edisto, Amelia on the Santee, or to Saxe-Gotha

6

on the Congaree, the Scotch-Irish who went to Williams-burg on the Black River, and the French Huguenots who went to New Bordeaux on Long Canes Creek—all passed through Charleston. They often arrived in "pitiful con-dition." In 1767 the church wardens of St. Philip's asked for subscriptions to take care of the Scotch-Irish who had arrived from Belfast. A captain had tried to bring 450 in his ship instead of the 200 who could have come in com-fort. Instead of berths nineteen inches wide for each person, the passengers scarcely had seven. Since the master had cut their provision allowances by almost three-quarters, a distemper had carried off upwards of 100 on the passage. Many children arrived without parents or relations. Among the township settlers only the Welsh, who came down from Pennsylvania to the Welsh Tract on the Pee Dee, did not pass through Charleston, although they did come to town eventually to establish their claims to land. Be-fore the 1750's the influx of settlers was from the coast inland; in the 1750's settlers moved down from the north overland; only after the 1770's did these "subsequent immi-grants" outnumber the "prior immigrants."

Sometimes these settlers passing through Charleston would drift back to town, like the DeSaussures from Pur-rysburg; and, in time, some of the sons of those who came from the north would seek their fortunes in the city, such as a Petigru or a Cheves. With all these people, there ex-isted a diversity of outlook and therefore an interweaving of countless ideas, ultimately a new culture. This mobility was a part of the fever of a frontier community, of which Charleston had many characteristics.

Charleston, although founded in 1670 and moved to its present location in 1680, did not begin to grow amazingly until the 1730's. It was situated in such a way that it would profit as soon as the surrounding country produced commodities for export. Although it was not located at the mouth of any of the three great river systems that flowed through South Carolina to the ocean (the Pee Dee, the Santee, and the Savannah, the red rivers that rise in the mountains, flow across the Piedmont, and sweep through the lowcountry to the sea), it did lie between two of the estuarial rivers that rise in the black-water swamps, the Ashley and the Cooper, and close to two others, the Stono and the Wando, and these gave it something of a hinterland. Charleston had a more extensive connection with the interior than either Georgetown or Beaufort: either by the old Indian path to the Cherokee country, which ran up Charleston Neck to Moncks Corner and then along the west side of the Santee past the Eutaws to Congaree Fort, then swung through Ninety-Six to Keowee and the Lower Towns of the Cherokees; or by the famous wagon road from Charleston to Philadelphia, which forked from the Cherokee Trail at Nelson's Ferry on the Santee and proceeded by way of Camden and the Waxhaws northward. Pack-horse trains brought fifty thousand deerskins annually to Charleston from the Indian nations and often, in the early days, Indians themselves as slaves for the West Indian market.

As the trade in deerskins declined and the trade in rice and indigo expanded, the inland waterways became the chief avenues to market. Thus, the location of Charleston at the center of an inland water system that stretched from the Cape Fear River in North Carolina to the St. John's River in Florida behind the sea islands was important. This was a natural waterway which needed only a few cuts, such as Wappoo Cut that connected the Stono and the Ashley opposite Charleston, to join in an almost continuous system. The only important internal improvement during the century before the coming of the railroad was the building and completion in 1800 of the Santee Canal, which joined the Cooper to the Santee and thus Charleston to the largest river system in South Carolina.

Charleston's commerce was supported by three crops grown in the lowcountry—first rice, then indigo, and finally sea island cotton. These were continuously supplemented by naval stores. Although rice was introduced in the 1690's, the clearing of the swamps and the diking of the marshes took many years, as did the effort to produce the best seeds and to find a suitable labor force. The solving of these problems coincided with the establishment of royal authority in the 1730's.

Those who began to plant rice in the 1730's had the best chance for quick and great profits. The independent traders, like Samuel and Joseph Wragg, had broken through the monopoly of the Royal African Company and were able, by that decade, to bring many cargoes of Negro slaves to Carolina, the first large influx. Colonial land policies crystallized at the same time, permitting the formation of plantations suitable for rice culture. In the 1730's the crown decided to honor patents (although not titles) for landgraves and caciques (orders of nobility instituted under the Proprietors) which confirmed great baronies in the hands of individual men. The headright system in South Carolina also permitted one man to accumulate large tracts of land, since a headright of fifty acres could be secured for each slave purchased. The first Thomas Lynch put together his Santee River properties by obtaining headrights of fifty acres each for every slave imported. Thus the Horrys, Lynches, and Allstons to the north and the Heywards, Barnwells, and Elliotts to the south of Charleston became great rice-planting families. They shipped their crops to Charleston by the inland waterways and followed for business and pleasure.

When indigo was introduced into South Carolina as a crop in the 1740's, the basis for a very important imperial agricultural commodity was laid. Indigo could be grown on the high land behind the rice fields as a supplementary crop to rice. Eliza Lucas solved the problem of preparing the commodity for market on her father's Stono River plantation, while Timothy Mellichamp perfected the culture of the crop on his Ashley River plantation. The choicest indigo was grown on the Black River above Georgetown, where in 1757 the Winyah Indico Society was formed to spread information on "Indico-making, from the cutting, to the barrelling."

Rice and indigo fitted in well with the British mercantile system. Neither could be grown in England, and not much indigo was grown in the British West Indies. Although rice was not consumed in great quantities in England, it could be shipped to Europe, where it was an important item of diet during times of short crops. Since indigo was needed by the developing British cloth industry, South Carolina was a favored child of England. In 1705, Parliament placed rice on the enumerated list, which meant that all rice must be shipped directly to England before going to any European destination; but, in 1730, Parliament made this restriction sit more easily upon the colony by exempting from this restriction shipments to ports south of Cape Finisterre. Indigo was favored by a Parliamentary bounty of six pence per pound in 1748, this being reduced to four pence per pound in 1770.

Sea island cotton was a development of post-Revolutionary society. South Carolina Tories who had fled to the Bahamas experimented with this staple, and information about the new crop filtered back to Carolina. With the invention of the cotton gin, the flow of both sea island cotton and upland cotton through Charleston reached a flood in the late 1790's. A bonanza period followed which lasted until 1819, when a decline in prices set in.

The growing of the crops concerned the province itself in which the planters were the main interest; the carrying of the crops concerned the city of Charleston in which the merchants were the key group. The latter began to wax rich and powerful in the 1730's. They developed business acumen which the merchants of Georgetown or Beaufort, Wilmington or Savannah were never able to challenge. In the 1760's the Charleston merchants gobbled up this southern trade as New York was to gobble up American trade in the 1820's.

The merchants emerged out of the factors sent to Charleston from Great Britain as agents of those who traded with the colonies. The factors came out to handle goods on commission, first the goods needed by the Indian traders, and then goods such as Negro cloth needed by the planters on their slave-operated plantations. As payment, they shipped back to their English merchants deerskins, rice, indigo, and occasionally specie which filtered in from the Spanish colonies to the southward. In time, after accumulating commissions, these agents might set themselves up as merchants, particularly after being situated in a port such as Charleston where so many rivulets of commerce merged into one oceanic stream. They then invested their own capital in the commerce of the port, they took the risks, and they began to accumulate great wealth.

The Charleston merchants sponsored storekeepers at the heads of navigation and at ferry crossings. From these they drew the items which were to be shipped overseas: naval stores from the Cape Fear, indigo from Georgetown, and rice from every river landing. These items were shipped to London, Bristol, Liverpool, and Glasgow, and to Cowes if destined for a Continental market at Rotterdam or Hamburg. "To Cowes and a market" became a Charleston colloquialism. Rice went directly to Lisbon and Oporto. In 1762 several cargoes of rice were sent to feed the Portuguese army encamped near Oporto. The returning vessels brought goods which were distributed through country outlets.

The Charleston merchant oligarchy had influence in the country parishes through the storekeepers. There were stores at Cainhoy on the Wando, at Moncks Corner and Childsbury (Strawberry Ferry) on the Cooper, at Dorchester (Bacon's Bridge) and Ashley Ferry Town (Shem Town) on the Ashley, at Rantowle's on the Stono, and at Jacksonborough on the Edisto. These were Charleston's satellite communities, which flourished as long as waterways were the important highways. They did not survive the eighteenth century.

At these towns country fairs were held for frolic and for profit. In 1723 three fairs were established on the Ashley and Cooper rivers. In April and May there would be fairs at Dorchester, Ashley Ferry Town, and Childsbury. Each would also have a fair in the fall. Slaves, cattle, horses, provisions, and other merchandise would be sold during the four-day fairs. All three fairs advertised in the *Gazette*, September 13, 1751, that there would be "some pretty diversions," which were obviously designed to bring in the customers. John Gordon advertised the Ashley Ferry fair for May, 1749, by announcing that "a very neat Saddle and Furniture, a pair silver spurs, and a handsome piece of useful Plate will be put up, *to be run for*, a very neat silver mounted Fowling-piece, *to be shot for*, a pair of silver mounted Pistols, *to be raffled for*, a Gold lac'd Hat *to be cudgelled for*, a Role of Tobacco and 3 Gross of Pipes, *to be grinn'd for by old Women*, a Pig soap'd all over *to be the Property of the Person that catches and holds it by the Tail. &c.* There will also be exhibited, a *Schara-mouche-Dance*, precisely at 3 o'Clock, by a Person from London. . . ." No one could be arrested by the civil authorities during the fair, and the Governor appointed a court of piepoudre to keep order during this time of mirth-making and merchandising.

James Crokatt, John Beswicke, John Nickleson, and Richard and Thomas Shubrick were excellent examples of the rising merchant class. James Crokatt, a Scotsman, was an Indian trader in Charleston and owner of Crokatt's Bridge, a wharf extending from Bay Street into the Cooper River. He served the city in several capacities, helped to found the Masons, made a fortune, and then, in 1739, retired to England, where after 1749 he served the colony as agent, being appointed after his successful effort to secure the bounty on indigo. His son-in-law John Nutt continued these commercial associations with Charleston until the end of the century. John Beswicke, who had earlier traded in North Africa, arrived in Charleston in 1734 as clerk of the market. Venturing into more lucrative lines, he too accumulated a fortune and returned to England in 1744, where he established a mercantile house, later taking as partners William Greenwood and his own nephew, William Higginson. Greenwood and Higginson, the surviving members of the firm, were the largest Carolina traders in London on the eve of the Revolution. John Nickleson and his wife's brothers, Richard and Thomas Shubrick, traded in Charleston under the partnership of Nickleson and Shubrick until the end of the 1740's when John Nickleson and Richard Shubrick moved to London. The *London Directory* of 1763 listed six firms as "Carolina Merchants": John Beswicke and Co., James and Charles Crokatt and Co., Grubb and Watson (both former partners of James Crokatt), Sarah Nickleson (the widow of John Nickleson), John Nutt, and Richard Shubrick. Their places of business were in Cheapside, Old Bethlem, Billiter Square, Cannon Street, and Barge Yard, Bucklesbury; their meeting place was the Carolina Coffee House in Birchin Lane. In each case these persons had had earlier connections with the colony, before they formed a group in London with a monopoly of the know-how for the Carolina trade.

In the 1740's it was the custom to go home once a fortune was made, and by that decade fortunes of ten to twenty thousand pounds sterling were not uncommon. These could be made in planting and in commerce. A writer to the *Gazette* in December, 1749, pointed out that "the Success of a Crokatt, a Shubrick, or a Beswicke, but a few years here in the Mercantile Way, or of a Lynch, or Huger, or a Serre, in the Planting Way, with many other such Instances, proves more in Favor of Carolina, than all the Pamphlets that were ever wrote about."

More and more, however, the merchants remained, lending their funds to young and enterprising new men and living off the returns. The interest rate had been 10 per cent, then dropped to 8 per cent in 1748, and to 7 per cent in 1777, a decline which was a sign of growing economic stability. Since the eighteenth-century ideal was the landed gentleman, there was a tendency for retiring merchants to become gentlemen-planters. A principal settlement of such was at Goose Creek, eighteen miles up the Neck from the city, rather reminiscent of clusters of London merchants at Hampstead or at Newington Green.

There were several groups in Charleston who served the merchants, principally the lawyers, the shipbuilders, and the mechanics. Lawyers were largely used in the securing of debts. Since the courts only met in Charleston, that was the place of residence of the entire legal profession. The fattest fees were earned by the lawyers who got the business of the largest London merchants.

There was always some shipbuilding in the vicinity of the harbor. There was a yard for many years on James Island, but the main center was at Hobcaw. John Rose, Clement Lempriere, and Robert Cochran built or repaired ships. The biggest ship built was *The Heart of Oak*, launched at John Rose's yard in 1763, a vessel of 180 tons with a capacity for one thousand barrels of rice. Of regular importance was the careening of ships to scrape the bottoms. Captain John Gascoigne, who had been sent out in 1727 to survey the coast, described in the logbook of the *Alborough* the manner in which his vessel was careened at Hobcaw. There were also yards at Georgetown early and at Beaufort later, but none of the Carolina shipyards could keep the British men-of-war properly fitted for sea. Captain Thomas Frankland took the HMS *Rose* in 1744

15

to Boston for major repairs, and all the captains took their ships to England for the best work.

The closest thing to a manufacturing establishment was James Reid's ropewalk, which employed a number of men who turned out the items necessary for outfitting a ship. There were various mechanics in the port: coopers, carpenters, bricklayers, silversmiths, goldsmiths, cabinetmakers, shipwrights, blacksmiths, brass founders, painters, shoemakers, and tailors. These men, who possessed ancillary skills needed in any great port, started out by using their hands, but after a time of some success they would secure apprentices and purchase slaves. They emerged as small entrepreneurs founding a business. Many graduated into the merchant class.

Upon the chaos of trade some order had to be established. In every youthful community dynamism had to give way to stability. In Charleston this stability was wrought first by the royal system of control as laid down by Parliament in the Navigation Acts and carried out in Charleston by the royal governor. In the second place, it was furthered by the local Commons House of Assembly, which governed the province and established the town commissions. Finally, true stability came through the natural evolution of Charleston society—by the formation of an elite through business and marriage ties that then exercised its influence through the private and social institutions of the city.

The royal governor was at the apex of each hierarchy designed to organize and stabilize society. As governor he was responsible to the crown for carrying out the Navigation Acts. He therefore watched over the collector of customs, the naval officer who kept the register of shipping, and the vice-admiralty court in which violations of the system were punished and where the prizes of the privateers were condemned. Although the Admiralty in London stationed naval vessels on the Carolina coast to watch over the system and protect trade, the captains of these ships did consult with the governors. The customs house on the bay, the vice-admiralty court in town, and the homes of the naval captains were all seats of royal power.

All land was held of the crown. The governor and Council issued the warrants of survey, and after the plats had been drawn by the surveyors, the governor and Council signed the grants. Each settler had to go to Charleston to find out whether his grant of land was legal. These procedures took place first in the surveyors's office, then in the Council chamber, and finally in the secretary's office, where the engrossed grants were filed. In 1731 the system by which the quit rents were collected was reorganized. The names of those who owed quit rents to the crown were recorded in the Memorial books, and henceforth the receiver general of quit rents sat in Charleston. The many transfers of town and country property were registered in the mesne conveyance office.

The governor appointed the justices of the peace, who exercised a local jurisdiction over crimes in the four counties. Major crimes were tried in the common law courts, that met in Charleston. Constables transported the charges and the prisoners to town. The provost marshal carried out the orders of the courts, sometimes by sending deputies through the length and breadth of the province. The only jail was in Charleston, to which the provost marshal held the keys.

The governor was commander-in-chief of the military forces in the province. These might consist of Regular troops from England, Independent companies, provincials, rangers, militia, or elite companies, all being used in colonial Carolina. Regulars were brought by Lieutenant-Colonel Henry Bouquet in 1757, and again in 1760 and 1761 by Colonel Archibald Montgomery and Colonel James Grant. Their red-coated uniforms could be seen in Charleston until 1769, when they were withdrawn. Independent companies had been organized in the 1740's under Colonel Alexander Vander Dussen to assist General James Oglethorpe against the Spaniards. They were not disbanded until 1764. Governor William Henry Lyttelton asked for provincials in 1759 in order to fight the Cherokees. Rangers were merely a light force of provincials used on the frontier. Lyttelton did much to invigorate the militia, largely intended for local defense, by personally attending the annual muster of each regiment in 1757. The best example of an elite company, a company which chose its own uniform and officers, was Christopher Gadsden's Artillery Company. The failure of the British to streamline this system forced them to rely upon Regulars in the colonies in the 1760's. The British interpreted the need as military weakness in the colonials, but they were mistaken.

The royal governor of South Carolina was also head of the Anglican church, which had been established in the province in 1706. He and the twenty-four lay commissioners were to make the appointments to the cures, but in practice this was taken out of their hands by the local vestries. The lay commissioners did meet annually in Charleston, at least to check the credentials of the arriving clergymen.

In spite of these great powers the governor was not all-powerful; he had to deal with and ask for the co-operation of the Assembly, which was elected by the people. The election law of 1721 had prescribed the qualifications for those who could vote for members and for those who could sit in the Assembly. To vote, one must be a free white man over twenty-one professing the Christian religion, must have been a resident of the colony for one year, and must possess a freehold of fifty acres or pay twenty shillings a year in provincial taxes. To be a member of the Assembly, one must have five hundred acres and ten slaves or houses and town lots worth one thousand pounds. That law had also divided representation among the parishes. St. Philip's parish was Charleston until 1751, when it was divided and St. Michael's parish formed out of the southern half of the city, that part which lay below Broad Street. St. Philip's parish sent five members to the Assembly until 1759, when St. Michael's (the church having been completed and a vestry elected) began to send three members and St. Philip's three. Since the Assembly met in Charleston and members did not have to reside in the parishes they represented, most of the members during the colonial period were Charlestonians, which quite often meant merchants. In 1741 an anonymous writer to the *Gazette* urged the election of merchants to the Assembly, particularly those who would continue to trade while they sat in the Assembly; the writer pointed out that the city of London sent four members who were invariably active trading men. "As we attempt to resemble *Great-Britain* in our political Government, so all laudable Practices of any Part of that Kingdom proper to be follow'd in this colony, ought certainly to be Examples to us."

The Assembly set the general property tax, the income tax, the export duties, and also the import duties on slaves.

They also appointed the officials who collected these taxes. In Charleston there was a set of provincial officials who collected the export tax and a set of royal officials who collected the royal import duties. The treasurer who kept these provincial taxes was the most important figure in the colony next to the governor. In time he became the appointee of the Assembly and answerable to that body for expenditures. Because he kept the funds in his personal possession, subject to a great bond, he was also the local banker, for there were no banks in Charleston until the 1790's. Gabriel Manigault and Jacob Motte, the two treasurers from 1735 to 1771, both grew vastly rich on the legal commissions.

Although Charleston was not incorporated until 1783, she had city government during the royal period. The Assembly set up commissions for certain civic purposes, provided the guidelines, and appointed the first members, but after the first year the members were elected annually on Easter Monday by the people of the town.

Five firemasters were elected annually. They were to inspect all buildings from time to time to see that a certain number of leather buckets and ladders were on hand. Theirs was an important task, and to this commission were elected the leading merchants of the city, who were continually re-elected. A law passed after the 1740 fire forbade the building of wooden houses, but this law was apparently not fully enforced.

There was more fluctuation in the membership of the commissioners of the streets and the commissioners of the workhouse and markets. These two commissions were staffed by merchants or by artisans. The commissioners of the streets were to supervise paving and cleaning. They also set the charges for haulage through the streets, the rates increasing as the distance from the wharves lengthened. Runaway apprentices and slaves might be held temporarily in the workhouse. If slaves were not called for within sixty days by an owner, they might be sold to pay for their room and board. There were a number of markets in town, supervised by a clerk of the market who collected the fees for stalls and enforced the sanitary regulations.

The packers and the wood and coal measurers were also established by the Assembly. The packers were more important, for they were to make certain that the exports measured up to Carolina quality. Those who usually held this position were the master coopers, the elite among the tradesmen. When an order might be made for repacking, or rebarreling, the cooper was the person with the skill for this job. The wood and coal measurers were assigned the duty of seeing that the townspeople were not overcharged for these necessities; coal came from England and wood from the surrounding countryside. These men were generally drawn from the artisan class.

Since the established church was responsible for certain civil functions, the churchwardens were important local officials. Primarily they had charge of the poor and could assess the people to contribute toward their support. Sometimes overseers of the poor were elected by the parishes to carry out these functions. Invariably the churchwardens of St. Philip's were the local merchants. They looked after apprentices, supervised indigent outpatients, and by 1738 opened a hospital. On a Sunday they might make a turn through the town in order to see that church was attended and no sports played. In 1747, Governor Glen backed up the churchwardens by appointing sentinels to stand at the town gates on Sunday to restrain loose and idle persons "from going a pleasuring on that Day during the Time of Divine Service" and to stop "all Drovers, Butchers and their Servants with their Carts or Horses from coming to Market on that Day."

All these commissioners and churchwardens served without pay. To serve was a duty that each civic-minded gentleman and artisan must accept. On the whole they did a good job. From time to time the grand jury would complain about certain failures; but then the grand jury was generally composed of these same men. Since men were fined for nonservice on grand and petit juries, those who refused to serve were known, and they were most often those called from the outlying districts. Thus the burden on the responsible classes in Charleston to serve on juries was great. In fact, they seemed to shoulder this burden for the entire province. A merchant oligarchy ruled the town and, to a great extent, the province.

Justice was harsh in the eighteenth century. Punishment was public and designed to fit the crime. Elizabeth Ward was fined five pounds proclamation money for selling beef by a false scale. Alexander Forbes was whipped at the cart's tail around Market Square for stealing a bridle and saddle. Dorothy Holmes was burned on the hand for stealing two silver waiters. James and Francis Scott were each burned on the left cheek and whipped at the cart's tail for stealing and killing cattle. Mary Stammers, who assaulted a constable in the execution of his office, was whipped at the gaol door. Forgers and counterfeiters stood in the pillory. Sarah Chamberlain suffered death for the murder of her bastard child; John Perrins, for bestiality. Thomas Ellis, alias "Stick in the Mud," was hanged for stealing a horse.

Negro slaves suffered death for arson and poisoning, the two crimes most feared by the white population. In 1741 a Negro slave was burned to death in Charleston for setting fire to a house. In October, 1749, the *Gazette* reported: "The horrid practice of poisoning white People, by the Negroes, has lately become so common, that with a few Days past, several Executions have taken Place in different Parts of the Country by burning, gibbeting, hanging, &c." In 1769 two slaves, Dolly and Liverpoole, were "burnt on the Work-house Green" for poisoning an infant, Dolly for administering the dose and Liverpoole for supplying the poison. The press gangs of His Majesty's ships contributed to the violence by seizing unsuspecting seamen when necessity demanded. When it was known that the men-of-war were short of crew, merchantmen headed upstream.

Above this turbulent and violent mass of humanity a South Carolina elite was forming. Marriage was the cement of the new society. The importance of family in the society and culture of Charleston cannot be overestimated, and it became highly important by mid–eighteenth century. The natural alliances at first were among the families of business partners or among the families of planters situated at some particular spot—such as at Winyah Bay, or on the Santee, or on the Cooper, or on the Edisto, or around Beaufort. But it was in Charleston that these separate familial groups became one through intermarriage. What drew them to Charleston was a common social life. Planters came to town for the season in late winter, for Charleston was very much like London. Every planter felt he should have a Charleston house, and most did. It was the center of trade, of law, of schooling, and of transportation to Europe. It may well have been the merchants who, acting as a catalyst, transformed these planting groups into one large low-country, or Charleston, society.

The parish records or the private journals of Mrs. Anne Manigault and of Colonel Isaac Hayne tell this story entry by entry. The large families of the prominent men speeded up the process. Benjamin Smith had twelve children by two wives; his brother Thomas, twelve by one wife. Eleanor Ball bore twelve children for Henry Laurens, dying at the birth of her last child. Jacob Motte, the treasurer, sired nineteen, of whom nine married. His sons-in-law were Thomas Shubrick, Thomas Lynch, William Moultrie, William Drayton, Dr. James Irving, Henry Peronneau, John Sandford Dart, and John Huger. The daughters of Jacob Bond of Hobcaw Point through their marriages unified the ship-building industry. Elizabeth Bond married, in 1745, Captain Richard I'On, master of a privateer; Susannah, in 1751, John Randall, an English mariner; Mary, before 1760, Job Milner, merchant of Charleston; Rebecca, in 1750, James Reid, the owner of the only ropewalk; Sarah, before 1750, Clement Lempriere, British naval officer turned ship-builder; Hester, in 1754, John Rose, who established Carolina's biggest shipyard; and Catherine, in 1759, Dr. Samuel Carne.

An elite was forming, and aristocracies tend to become rigid and to solidify. Only unusual factors prevent an aristocracy from becoming a caste, which is an elite that has withdrawn from power, adopting an exclusive attitude toward others, retreating into private clubs, refusing, above all, to take in new members. The Carolina aristocracy was never a caste in the eighteenth century; it was always at the center of power and quite willing to absorb new talent. Many tradesmen joined the elite in the eighteenth century:

Thomas Heyward, the hatter; John Rose, the shipwright; Daniel Cannon, the carpenter. But what kept the society open in the eighteenth century were the new avenues to wealth continually opened up by the wars of that century.

II.

The Open City

IT WAS THE VIOLENCE of eighteenth-century life that kept Charleston society fluid. Disease, fires, hurricanes, and wars kept the people from settling down to a long-term routine. Life was short, and mortality high. A large progeny was the best insurance for the continuation of the family line. Henry Laurens lost seven of his twelve children before his wife died. He himself outlived all except three. If there were only a few children, a family might fail of establishment. James Parsons, as famous a lawyer as John Rutledge and Charles Pinckney, left no heirs, for his two sons predeceased him. When his second son died in 1778 "in the bloom of youth," the *South-Carolina and American General Gazette* commented: "The situation of his disconsolate parents, thus bereaved of their only hope, may be conceived, but language would fail to describe it."

Malaria and yellow fever were constantly present in Charleston, but smallpox, an intermittent visitor, was the most devastating disease. On April 13, 1738, the ship *London Frigate* arrived from Guinea with a cargo of slaves. Some of those sold into the country had smallpox, and shortly thereafter, an outbreak took place in various parts of the colony. The Rev. George Whitefield wrote home that the disease had "spread so extensively that there were not a sufficient number of persons in health to attend the sick, and many persons perished from neglect and want . . . ." After an outbreak of smallpox at Fort Prince George in December, 1759, Lyttelton's returning army brought the disease to Charleston. This was the most widespread and deadly of the colonial epidemics; not even inoculation could stem the ravages of the disease. From the most unfortunate slave to the wife of the speaker of the Assembly, many died. The Assembly itself had to adjourn to Ashley Ferry Town to continue its session.

The fear of infection from the newly arriving Negro or the visiting stranger (on one occasion whooping cough had been traced to a New Yorker) forced the province to establish rigorous quarantine regulations. No vessel with Negroes from Africa could pass Fort Johnson into Ashley or Cooper rivers until the Negroes had been landed for ten days on Sullivan's Island, during which period the slaves and ships were cleansed. A pesthouse was built on Sullivan's Island which, when Pelatiah Webster visited it in 1765, was fitted "with pretty good conveniences." There were at that time two to three hundred Negroes undergoing quarantine for smallpox on the sandy, hot, barren island. "The most moving sight was a poor white man performing quarantine alone in a boat at anchor ten rods from shore with an awning & pretty poor accomodations." In 1769 a sea captain had apparently thrown overboard a number of dead Negroes, whose bodies drifted onto the marsh opposite the town. The Governor offered one hundred pounds in the *Gazette*, June 8, 1769, to anyone who would give information leading to the conviction of those responsible for this hazard to local health.

It is a wonder that Charleston still looks like an eighteenth-century city for it has suffered grievously from great fires. On November 18, 1740, a fire broke out at the corner of Broad and Church streets, and, fanned by a northwest wind, burned for six hours, consuming all the houses and stores down to Granville's Bastion, "which was the most valuable part of the Town on account of the Buildings and Trade." The fire also burned the west side of Church Street from Broad to Tradd, Colonel Miles Brewton's house below being saved by the sailors of the royal naval vessels who gave help "in pulling down and blowing up Houses." The loss was estimated at 300 houses. Parliament itself appropriated £20,000 sterling for the 171 sufferers. On January 15, 1778, another fire in the same area consumed 250 houses. This fire started at Queen and Church streets and burned down to Stoll's Alley. Elkanah Watson, in town on a visit to Nathaniel Russell, commented: "Many who, a few hours before, retired to their beds in affluence, were now reduced, by the all-devouring element, to indigence." On June 13, 1796, a fire burned a wide swath from the market at Broad and Meeting streets to Cumberland and State, reputedly consuming 500 houses. In the nineteenth century there were other devastating conflagrations.

Between the fires came the hurricanes, whose paths always skirted the western fringes of the Bermuda High and thus quite often thundered into Charleston. An early hurricane of 1686 actually saved the city from destruction by disrupting Spanish plans for invasion, but in 1752 two severe storms swept over Charleston.

On September 15, 1752, the winds blew at hurricane force from four in the morning until nine, "when the flood came in like a bore, filling the harbor in a few minutes: Before 11 o'clock, all the vessels in the harbor were on shore, except the Hornet man-of-war, which rode it out by cutting away her main-mast; all the wharves and bridges were ruined, and every house, store, &c. upon them beaten down, and carried away (with all the goods, &c. therein)

. . . and great quantities of merchandise, &c. in the stores on Bay-street damaged, by their doors being burst open: The town was likewise overflowed, the tide or sea having rose upwards of Ten feet above the high-water mark at spring-tides, and nothing was now to be seen but ruins of houses, canows, wrecks of pettiaugers and boats, masts, yards, incredible quantities of all sorts of timber, barrels, staves, shingles, household and other goods, floating and driving, with great violence, thro' the streets, and round about the town. The inhabitants, finding themselves in the midst of a tempestuous sea, the wind still continuing, the tide (according to its common course) being expected to flow 'till after one o'clock, and many of the people already being up to their necks in water in their houses; began now to think of nothing but certain death: But . . . they were soon delivered from their apprehensions; for, about 10 minutes after 11 o'clock, the wind veered to the E. S. E., and S. W., very quick, and then . . . the waters fell about 5 feet in the space of 10 minutes, without which unexpected and sudden fall, every house and inhabitant in this, must, in all probability, have perished."

As it was, many drowned. The pesthouse on Sullivan's Island was swept away. One ship with a cargo of Palatines was driven from her anchorage "into the marsh near to James Island where, by continual rolling the passengers were tumbled from side to side. About twenty of them, by bruises and other injuries, lost their lives." It was necessary to dig a channel one hundred yards long, thirty-five feet wide, and six feet deep, in order to drag the ship off the marsh. Another terrible hurricane struck the city just fifteen days later.

From time to time ships were lost at sea. Many passengers

who sailed from Charleston never reached their destinations. Miles Brewton and his family disappeared in 1775. Clement Lempriere, Thomas Lynch, Jr., and Peter Timothy, on separate voyages, were lost at sea during the Revolution. And in 1812 the ship on which Theodosia Burr Alston sailed from Georgetown vanished off Cape Hatteras.

Fire and marine insurance were available, but the rates were high. In 1735 the Friendly Society for the Mutual Insuring of Houses against Fire was formed in Charleston, the first fire insurance company in America. But the company went bankrupt when it could not meet the claims arising out of the fire of 1740. Marine insurance was written by groups of local merchants or by London underwriters. It was not until the 1790's that a marine insurance company was formed in Charleston. During the wars freight rates climbed rapidly, making it unprofitable to ship bulky commodities such as rice. There was no life insurance.

Fires and hurricanes and individual disasters had only temporary effects upon the commerce of the port; but the wars had more lasting effects. A hurricane might open a new entry across the bar, but a war might open an entirely new avenue of commerce. The wars were, therefore, the fertilizing agents in the life of the city: the War of Jenkins' Ear from 1739 to 1748, the Great War for Empire from 1754 to 1763, the American Revolution from 1775 to 1783, and finally the French Revolution and the Wars of Napoleon from 1793 to 1815. Charleston was involved in war either directly or indirectly during almost half of her golden century. It was amid these four world-wide struggles that Charleston fought for a place in the Atlantic commercial world, giving strength to her men and fusing all her citizens into one culture. Static tendencies could not triumph as long as the wars lasted. It took a very clever man with some luck to ride out the shifting fortunes of war. William Pinckney went bankrupt for a large sum in the 1740's; John Stuart and Daniel LaRoche failed to survive the 1750's. A sudden shift in the price of rice in 1796 toppled several Charleston firms, and the Peace of Amiens in 1802 brought down the great Anglo-Carolina firm of Bird, Savage, and Bird.

As news of declarations of war was always slow in arriving, Charleston lived in a continuous state of "cold war," her citizens suffering many irritations before they knew that they might retaliate. One of these irritations, the cutting off of Captain Jenkins' ear by the captain of a Spanish *guarda-costa* in the Straits of Florida, eventually brought on the war with Spain in 1739. But this war was not proclaimed in Charleston until April 28, 1740, when it was formally announced, as was the custom, in four public places: at the Council chamber, in the public market place, at Broughton's Battery, and at Granville's Bastion. General James Oglethorpe, who had been placed in supreme command of the Georgia and Carolina forces, organized the attack against the Spaniards. In the joint expedition against St. Augustine in 1740, Colonel Alexander Vander Dussen led the Carolina troops, while Captain Thomas Frankland marshaled the British naval vessels to assist in the blockading of the city. This expedition to take St. Augustine failed, but Oglethorpe secured the southern frontier by his victory on St. Simon's Island in July, 1742.

On July 23, 1744, the war against the King of France was proclaimed in the formal fashion in Charleston. Since the remainder of this war was fought on the sea, Charleston merchant vessels were convoyed to England by His Majesty's naval vessels, which were frequently returning to England after service on the Carolina station. The British naval officers were the most romantic group in the port, and none more so than Captain Thomas Frankland of the HMS *Rose*. Frankland, a direct descendant of that unyielding fighter Oliver Cromwell, made many cruises to the southward, scouring the Caribbean and bringing home to Charleston his many prizes. The *Gazette*, in 1741, described a few of the Spanish craft that swarmed in the Gulf Stream off the coast of Cuba. There were a number of sloops and schooners: one with "her Sides painted blue, and Streaks yellow"; another, about one hundred tons, "having 120 Men, 14 Carriage Guns 6 Pounders, and 14 Swivels, a high cocked up Head, a wastle cloth all round to hide her Ports, freezed with black and yellow Paint, her Oars upon the Quarter"; and a settee with "a high cocked narrow Pink stern." From time to time, Frankland brought into Charleston some of these vessels as prizes, which were then condemned in the vice-admiralty court. Spanish coffee and French sugars with gold and silver coins then filtered through the business of the port. The grateful Charleston merchants presented Frankland with a silver bowl for stimulating trade, and the mechanics subscribed a poem to him: "Below our Bay you make their Vessels ride, / stripp'd of their Riches, and all Spanish pride." With his share of the prize money he bought a wharf which became a depot for his later captures. In May, 1743, he married Sarah Rhett, "a beautiful and accomplish'd young Lady, with a large Fortune," and the granddaughter of Colonel William Rhett, who had earlier fought the pirates. Frankland's home became the center of all that was rich and romantic about the city.

His greatest prize was the four-hundred-ton ship *Conception*, which he captured off the west end of Cuba in December, 1744. It was a twenty-gun French ship carrying 326 men, including the passengers, and traveling from Carthagena to Havana. As the *Gazette* reported, it had been difficult for the crew to ascertain just how much gold and silver had been taken. The ship had "on board 800 serons of Cocoa, in each of which 'tis said is deposited as customary a Bar of Gold, 68 Chests of Silver Coins (already found) containing 310,000 Pieces of Eight, private adventures in Gold and Silver Coins, and wrought Plate of equivalent Value . . . a compleat Set of Church Plate, a large Quantity of Gold Buckles and Snuff-Boxes, a curious Two-wheel'd Chaise of Silver, the wheels, axles, &c. all of the same Metal, a large Quantity of Diamonds, Pearl, and other Precious Stones, upwards of 600 Weight of Gold, &c and fresh Discoveries are daily made of more Treasure. 'Tis impossible to give an Exact Account of what is on board this Prize, some Gold having been secreted even in the Knees, Barricado, &c the Heels of the Prisoners Shoes having been made hollow, were also full of Gold." The officers and crew presented to Captain Frankland's lady the silver chaise "as a Testimony of Gratitude to that Brave Commander." Another poem appeared in the *Gazette* on this occasion, entitled "Victorious Frankland, Carolina's Pride": "By Every Chief if Feats like this were done, / Peru and Mexico would be our own."

Although Carolina often obtained specie in this manner, most of it was shipped to England. On June 1, 1745, when the HMS *Rose* and the HMS *Flamborough* sailed for England as convoy for a fleet of merchant vessels, the newspaper noted: "The *Rose* Man-of-War is reckon'd to be the richest English Ship (with Gold and Silver, &c.) that has sail'd from America: and *Flamborough* has a considerable quantity of money on board." Half way over, the *Rose* left the merchant vessels, laden with rice worth £20,000 sterling belonging to George Austin, Benjamin Smith, and others, and set out ahead for England. When Frankland was criticized for abandoning the merchant vessels, he pointed to his need to safeguard £80,000 sterling of gold and silver on board his own ship. Although Frankland was stationed in the Caribbean during the next war, he eventually settled down as a Yorkshire squire, well endowed with the fortunes of war to sustain the baronetcy he inherited upon his elder brother's death.

During this war Charleston merchants bought vessels condemned by the vice-admiralty courts in Charleston and in New Providence and fitted them out as privateers, hoping to secure some of the rich booty for themselves. With the slave trade shut off in 1740 as an aftermath of the Stono Rebellion of 1739 and with the rice trade suffering from very high wartime insurance rates, the servicing of naval vessels and the sending out of privateers opened new lines of endeavor. But the introduction of indigo represented the permanent boost to trade provided by this war. With the Spanish and French sources for indigo cut off, it was an auspicious time to begin the production of indigo in Carolina. Behind the barrier of war the crop caught on, and in 1748, as the war ended, the grant of the Parliamentary bounty saved the crop. Henry Laurens wrote Sarah Nickleson, August 1, 1755: " 'Twas entirely owing to the last War that we became an Indigo Country & we hope a new war will learn us how to propagate some other useful Articles which would not be attempted with any Spirit whilst the Planter can find his Account in continuing in the old Tract."

Although the Great War for the Empire did not provide Carolinians with a new staple, that war did not disrupt the trade in rice and indigo. Since the English dominated the sea lanes during this war to a greater extent than in the last, freight rates were not as high. Rice continued to be shipped, the slave trade flourished, and indigo planters reaped bonanza profits. Although privateering was not as important during this war, the arrival of Regular troops in Charleston with supply needs stimulated the economy.

The fighting began on the Ohio River. When Governor Robert Dinwiddie called on Governor Glen for assistance in fighting the French and Indians, Glen sent to Virginia Captain James Mackay's Independent Company, men who had seen service under Oglethorpe. After Lieutenant Peter Mercier lost his life at Great Meadows on the Ohio, his frontier exploits were recalled in the *Gazette*:

> *By all esteem'd, admir'd, extoll'd, approv'd.*
> *In death lamented, as in life belov'd:*
> *Georgia loud-sounding thy achievements tell,*
> *And sad Virginia marks where Mercier fell.*

To meet the threat on the frontier, Governor Glen built Fort Prince George in the Lower Towns of the Cherokees and Fort Loudoun in the Overhill Towns. These were garrisoned by Independent companies under the command of Lieutenant Raymond DeMere and Lieutenant John Stuart. The defenses of Charleston herself were strengthened by the engineer William Gerard de Brahm, working under the direction of the commissioners of fortifications. When

Lieutenant-Colonel Henry Bouquet brought British Regulars to Charleston in 1757, the commissioners built barracks for them on the Free School lands. These preparations, financed by additional taxation, were fortunately completed by 1759, when Carolina was faced with the Cherokee rebellion, the last serious Indian threat to the province and the city.

It took three expeditions to subdue and crush the Cherokees. Governor William Henry Lyttelton, eager for fame and glory and thinking little of the obstacles in his way, called out the militia and raised provincial forces. Marching by way of Moncks Corner, the Congarees, and Ninety-Six, Lyttelton reached Fort Prince George, where he made a treaty with the Indians, hastily drawn because the term of enlistment of his troops was to run out shortly. His expedition was more disaster than success, since he brought back smallpox, not peace. In 1760, Colonel Archibald Montgomery was sent by General Jeffrey Amherst on a summer campaign. He landed his forces up the Cooper River at Moncks Corner and followed the same route to the Cherokee country. Because of haste, he, like Braddock, was ambushed in a narrow defile where his troops could not be properly deployed.

The conqueror of the Cherokees was Colonel James Grant in the successful expedition of 1761. This time Colonel Thomas Middleton, with the assistance of Lieutenant-Colonel Henry Laurens, led the provincials, who accompanied Colonel James Grant's Regulars. They marched up and back a third time, but this time they laid waste fifteen Indian towns of the lower and middle settlements. The tensions of that quick, vigorous, cruel campaign erupted into a number of personal encounters. Although it was a training ground for many who would distinguish themselves during the Revolution, such as William Moultrie and Francis Marion, it was also the breeding ground of personal feuds, most notably that between Henry Laurens and Christopher Gadsden, once friends, later foes.

These expeditions not only punished the Indians but also brought the backcountry to life. To organize three successive expeditions, it was necessary to marshal wagon trains, to buy foodstuffs, to stimulate overproduction. This was done under the direction of the Commissary General, William Pinckney, and the contractors for the British army, Joseph Nutt and Benjamin Stead. These expeditions, in providing the backcountry with a market, aroused the settlers and taught them lawlessness. The Cherokee war provided the background for the Regulator movement, which was the first significant pressure of the back settlements upon Charleston.

South Carolinians anxiously followed the war in Canada and in the West Indies. In October, 1758, there was much feasting and drinking, firing of guns, and beating of drums by the New Englanders who had settled on the Edisto, near Jacksonborough, to celebrate the victory at Louisbourg. A year later, the *Gazette* of October 27, 1759, ran what was almost a headline for an eighteenth-century newspaper: "God be praised! QUEBEC is in *English* Hands." But even more interest was attached to the victories in the West Indies. The capture of Guadeloupe in 1759 opened up a new market for rice. When the troops of Colonel Grant had finished their job in the mountains, they were sent to Charleston and transported to the West Indies to take part in the reduction of Martinique and Dominica. With the capture of Martinique, the *Gazette* announced that "the French Power in America" was "thereby effectually crushed." News soon followed that Havana had been taken by the Earl of Albemarle. Thus two more markets for Carolina rice were opened, and they remained open even though the three large islands were returned to France and Spain at the end of the war, because Parliament, in 1764, permitted rice to be shipped to these foreign islands thereafter.

Markets for rice and indigo had grown during the war, and planters were eager for slaves. Since the troops had to be fed and supplied with barrack "necessaries," the local economy had boomed. A new set of fortunes had, therefore, been made. Benjamin Smith, who had inherited James Crokatt's business, had made a trip to England in 1752 to establish his credit and to secure a new supply of goods. Upon returning after the great hurricanes of that year, he had traded on his own. When he began to import slaves, he took as a partner the young Miles Brewton. Henry Laurens, who had learned the business of trade as an apprentice in the house of Crokatt in London, had formed a partnership with George Austin in 1749, after making a tour of London, Bristol, and Liverpool to establish contacts. In 1757, Austin and Laurens had added Austin's nephew, George Appleby, to the firm. The firms of Smith and Brewton and of Austin, Laurens, and Appleby were the leading importers of slaves and goods during this war. At the end of the war the partnerships were dissolved, the men retiring from trade. Austin and Appleby went to England, but Benjamin Smith bought Accabee on the Ashley, and Laurens bought Mepkin on the Cooper. At this time more of the retiring merchants remained in the province.

The end of the Great War for Empire brought a feeling

of security. The Cherokees, the French, and the Spaniards had been defeated. Although Cuba had been returned to her, Spain lost East and West Florida to England. England also obtained the Neutral Islands (St. Vincent, Dominica, Tobago) and Grenada. South Carolina, therefore, began to take advantage of these new opportunities by developing her lands between the Altamaha and the St. John's, by sending her sons to East and West Florida, and by opening up new trade ties with the Neutral Islands and Grenada. During the first postwar year the *Gazette* recorded almost daily arrivals of men ready to start out in trade. Some young men had advantages. The sons of Benjamin and Thomas Smith, Thomas Loughton Smith and Roger Smith, were just beginning a mercantile career. The former apprentices of Henry Laurens, William Price and John Hopton, armed with letters of introduction, made the circuit of the Atlantic Basin to establish contacts and, in 1764, set up a firm in Charleston. The governor of East Florida, Colonel James Grant, had many friends in Charleston, among them being Henry Laurens. Soon many Scotsmen were passing through on their way to Florida; a Glasgow newspaper advertised ships to Charleston whence by easy voyage the new lands in Florida could be reached. This new push of empire evolved into the crisis that brought on the American Revolution.

Why should men who had prospered from the British imperial system and who stood to prosper in the future take the road to independence? Two recent books have attempted to answer that question. Eugene Sirmans, in his history of colonial South Carolina to 1763, describes a growing unity. The South Carolinians had first divided over the question of religion, but this issue had been put to rest in 1706 with the establishment of the Church of England. The Huguenots had been comprehended, and the dissenters gradually pacified. The next great divisive issue was the paper-money question, the merchants favoring paper tied firmly to sterling and the planters favoring more paper, regardless of depreciation. During Governor Robert Johnson's regime, the depreciation of paper money had been stopped and pegged seven to one to sterling, a moderate compromise which lasted until the Revolution. From 1743 to 1763 the principal story concerned the aspirations of the members of the Commons House of Assembly. During this period that body consolidated its power at the expense of the royal governor and the royal Council. The Assembly built itself a new State House in the 1750's and began consciously to copy the forms of the English House of Commons. The members secured a mace and a complete set (with index) of the journals of the English House of Commons for their State House library. As Jack Greene has pointed out in *The Quest for Power*, by 1763 the local oligarchy had won its claim to power. Its pretensions must henceforth be respected. When one considers that by 1763 this aristocracy was immensely rich and immensely secure, because of the removal of the French from the Ohio, the crushing of the Indians, and the removal of the Spaniards from the southward, then one can understand this self-confidence.

The men who became the greatest patriots were excellent examples of this new assertiveness. Henry Laurens was busy buying plantations in South Carolina and in Georgia and building a great townhouse amid a four-acre garden. Thomas Lynch, the successful rice planter from the banks of the Santee, married the daughter of the treasurer, Jacob

Motte. John Rutledge, fresh from his studies in London, became the leading lawyer almost overnight. Christopher Gadsden, who had made one fortune by 1761, closed his stores at the Cheraws and in Georgetown and began to build the largest wharf in America and to develop a suburb just north of town.

Nothing did more to make the new men suspicious of the crown than the arrival of placemen. Peter Leigh superseded Charles Pinckney in the 1750's as chief justice. In the 1760's his son Egerton Leigh, the beau ideal of the placemen, replaced John Rutledge as attorney-general and soon held many royal offices. The attempt of the royal governor, Boone, to prevent Gadsden from taking his seat in the Assembly was the most direct threat to the pretensions of these men. When Daniel Moore arrived in 1766 to take the place of the late and well-beloved Hector Berenger de Beaufain, who had been collector of the customs for thirty-three years, the conspiracy against local officeholders became more apparent. When all the assistant judges were swept aside and royal appointees took their places, the evidence was thought to be conclusive.

The Sugar Act did not bear heavily upon Carolina, and the Stamp Act was not openly opposed by some of the leading citizens, but John Rutledge, the lawyer, Thomas Lynch, the planter, and Christopher Gadsden, the merchant, were sent to the Stamp Act Congress in New York and were much honored upon their return. Yet that crisis revealed some of the dangers the rich and the wellborn might have to face in case of rebellion. Laurens' new home was invaded by the mob in search of stamps. There was also a rumor that there would be a slave rebellion at Christmas time, when slaves were given a little freedom for fes-

41

tivities. Since eight thousand slaves had been imported in 1765, three times the annual importation, Lieutenant-Governor William Bull was forced to alert the masters of the vessels in the harbor, very numerous at the time because of the impossibility of finding clearances as long as stamps were not used, to have their men ready to land and to defend the town. As a means of ferreting out the ringleaders, Catawba Indians, by a promise of bounties for scalps, were brought down from the backcountry to hunt down the runaway slaves in the surrounding swamps who were thought to be urging on the revolt. Over such tumult would rich men dare to revolt and open up the seams of society?

It was the Townshend duties and accompanying regulations that brought a change of heart in merchants like Laurens. His personal dispute with Daniel Moore was symbolic. Laurens, busily developing his newly acquired Georgia lands, sent his coasting schooners to bring his produce to Charleston and to supply his plantations. Such vessels, used by every great merchant and large planter, had been free from regulations, but the new regulations were designed to trap them. There was a rush to register these coasting vessels in May, 1767, but Laurens was already caught in the toils of the official regulations. Irked, he twisted Moore's nose one day while walking on the Battery. A pamphlet war ensued, in which Henry Laurens, Gabriel Manigault, and their friends were pitted against the placemen, Daniel Moore and Egerton Leigh.

The attempt of the British to force troops on the Carolinians aggravated this situation. There was a quarrel in Charleston over "barrack necessaries," just as there was in New York. Should the Assembly appropriate funds for candles, bedding, beer, and other essentials for the Regulars stationed in the Charleston barracks? Should she pay for the transportation of supplies to the frontier forts? Fortunately the troops were withdrawn from Charleston in 1769 as part of the decision to concentrate the British forces into key posts. Their departure may have prevented a "Charleston Massacre."

Many men, knowing their English and European history, and having read the Irish, Scottish, and dissenting writers, began to perceive in these events a distinct conspiracy against their liberties. Those who had been meeting under the liberty tree and in the taverns now found allies in the counting houses. Thus, in the summer of 1769, a committee of thirty-nine was formed, thirteen from each of the groups in the city, merchants, planters, and artisans, to enforce a nonimportation agreement against England. When the Assembly appropriated 1,500 pounds sterling in December, 1769, as a gift to John Wilkes, the crown, in order to punish the Assembly, brought its business to a virtual halt. When the Governor moved the meeting place of the Assembly from Charleston to Beaufort in 1772, he sealed the doom of the royal cause. Was Charleston no longer to be the capital of the province?

It was the threat of monopoly control for a few favored merchants as well as the question of taxation that drove Charlestonians to seize the tea and store it in the basement of the new customs house. Roger Smith, William Greenwood, and Peter Leger, the consignees of the tea, bowed to the will of the townsmen. It was not until the townsmen began to enforce the Association adopted at Philadelphia in October, 1774, that a few citizens joined the placemen to oppose the almost unanimous citizens. Some, like William Wragg, were banished to their plantations; others, like Miles Brewton, sailed away. But, within the city, the placemen were silenced and excluded from public life.

Lord William Campbell, who arrived in June, 1775, in HMS *Scorpion*, had a chance to arouse the backcountry against the lowcountry, for emissaries sought him out for advice. But on September 15, 1775, Lord William had to steal from his home on lower Meeting Street, by the rear water entrance, and row out to HMS *Tamar*, anchored in Rebellion Road. Such interference with royal authority would obviously have to be punished. As the fleet of Sir Peter Parker and the army of Sir Henry Clinton drew near in the late spring of 1776 (Lord William had gone to meet them), the Carolinians built a new fort of logs on Sullivan's Island, as well as additional fortifications at Haddrell's Point. Fort Sullivan (later to be named Fort Moultrie after its victorious defender Colonel William Moultrie) was to continue as a new feature of the harbor landscape, and the palmetto logs that had absorbed the full power of the British fleet were to be a new symbol for the state. But the failure of the British at Fort Moultrie altered the life of the city very little except in a psychological sense. It gave the citizens confidence and enhanced their pride. It gave them symbols for their new state—palmettos, a flag, and Sergeant Jasper.

Just as the Charlestonians slipped free of British control, they introduced a new element into the government of the state and life of the city, the influence of the backcountry. In the Circuit Court Act of 1769 the Assembly had provided jails and courthouses for the backcountry. By 1772 this new system of justice was functioning. But there was no addition of representation until the Provincial Con-

44

gresses were called to meet in Charleston. To these came men who had been to Charleston before as constables, deputy surveyors, bounty petitioners, or supplicants at court, and not as they came now, the equal of the merchants and the planters. The first state constitution, written in 1776, did not satisfy these new men. Therefore, in 1777, it was re-written to bring about some of the reforms desired, particularly the disestablishment of the Anglican church. A new constitution of 1778 appeared with these concessions, the price that the merchant oligarchy paid for the help of the new men and an extension of Carolina solidarity to the upcountry.

It was at the time of these constitutional changes, in February, 1777, that an oath was prescribed as a sign of loyalty to the new state. Those who refused to "acknowledge [that] the State of South Carolina is and of right ought to be a free, independent, and sovereign state" were banished, being given one year in which to sell their lands and remove their property. Some seventy-five men were banished.

For a while the sorting out had been done; those who remained turned their attentions to wartime opportunities. Shipments of arms, ammunition, and supplies for the Continental army arrived direct from France and Holland. Privateers were sent out under letters of marque issued by the new state. A South Carolina navy was acquired. Continental vessels stopped by on the way to West Indian missions. Much of the new wealth was loaned to the state. Therefore, even though these profiteers might waver in 1780, 1781, and 1782, they had reasons to hope for the success of the new state.

In 1780, Sir Henry Clinton moved to cut off this lucrative trade, and to raise the backcountry for the English cause. Sir Henry, in February, 1780, landed a large force south of Charleston, this time bringing enough troops to invest the city in the manner he found most suitable. His step-by-step investiture was, in a sense, a tour of the outlying areas of Charleston. He landed on Seabrook's Beach, marching across Johns Island to James Island, where he established himself at Peronneau's house near Wappoo Cut on the Stono River. The British then moved from the south side of Wappoo Cut on the Stono to the north side of the Cut on the Ashley, where, at Fenwick's Point, they constructed a battery. They marched up the west side of the Ashley to Lining's house on Lining's Creek and then to Ashley Ferry Town near Drayton Hall, whence they crossed to Gibbs Landing on Charleston Neck.

By this time Charleston, which had outgrown the walled city of 1704, had become another fortified city of greater extent. Upon each tongue of land penetrating the marshes of the Ashley and Cooper rivers, batteries were placed. The main line of fortifications crossed the Neck just north of Boundary Street. A wet ditch, dug between the Ashley and the Cooper just north of the line, strengthened the defenses. The British, guided by their corps of engineers, built parallels, sapped, and mined, until two series of fortifications faced each other across the peninsula. The British had taken the only rise in land on the Neck, Hampstead, and from that vantage point Clinton could survey the scene.

Meanwhile, Admiral Mariot Arbuthnot had entered the harbor—Forts Johnson and Moultrie being eventually taken —but he could not advance his ships up the Cooper River, since the Carolinians had sunk ships between the town and

Shute's Folly to block his way. The one escape route for the Americans was up the Wando River, which joins the Cooper across from Charleston. To block this route, Clinton sent Lord Cornwallis to the head of the Cooper River navigation, Biggin Bridge, then to Cainhoy on the Wando, and Lempriere's shipyard near Mount Pleasant. The bombardment was not ruthless, and the city was not destroyed. Clinton wanted to use the port as his headquarters. The fall of Charleston on May 12, 1780, was the greatest victory for the British in the Revolution.

A civil war followed. Clinton first paroled those whom he had captured in the city and then almost immediately began to demand their allegiance and support. Some were willing to sign congratulations to Clinton for his taking of Charleston and to Cornwallis for his victory in August at Camden, but others used their influence to prevent any cooperation with the British. Because these men undermined the attempts of the British to organize loyalist regiments, the British authorities rounded up the most prominent of the patriots (many were dragged to the prison under the Exchange at night) and shipped them off to St. Augustine for safekeeping. Patriots from the outlying parishes were sent to the sea islands south of Charleston. The captured soldiers were interned at Haddrell's Point; the officers were held at Charles Pinckney's Snee Farm in Christ Church parish. Some were also retained on the *Pack Horse* and the *Torbay*, prison ships in the harbor.

In the city, with the commanders ensconced in the Miles Brewton mansion and other homes commandeered for the British officers, the pressure was on taking protection. One could not use the court established under the Board of Police otherwise. As the British began to confiscate prop-

47

erty, those who feared for their property complied. Since Charleston was the base from which to supply the British forces in the field, merchants came out from England to service the forces. Others, like John Tunno and John Champneys, who had refused to take the oath of 1777, came back. Although some of the former royal officials returned, royal government was not re-established in South Carolina as it was in Georgia. The Board of Police operated under the direction of Lieutenant-Colonel Nisbet Balfour and then under General Alexander Leslie.

The period of occupation, the most romantic period of Charleston's history, was a time of noble deeds and mysterious actions. The hanging of Colonel Isaac Hayne, who had given his word and then had taken up the sword again, was the *cause célèbre*. And thus, this period has been used as the subject of many novels. Rafael Sabatini in *The Carolinian*, Gwen Bristow in *Celia Garth*, and William Gilmore Simms in *The Partisan*, *The Forayers*, *Eutaw*, *Katherine Walton*, and *Mellichampe* portrayed the drama of the times. Such historical novels actually give a better picture of the times than do the history books, for novels always have characters on each side in varying walks of life, while history books have often portrayed the struggle as merely right against wrong.

As General Nathanael Greene hemmed the British into Charleston and its environs after his battle at Eutaw Springs in September, 1781, the British resorted to raids up each river and along the coast in order to secure the foodstuffs needed for their garrison. Greene tried to hold the towns at the heads of navigation, Cainhoy, Biggin Bridge, Dorchester, Rantowle's, and Jacksonborough. Francis Marion parried raids on the Santee, while John Laurens was killed at Combahee Bluff by a British raiding party. Greene watched all from Round O. In order to put pressure upon the men in Charleston, the patriots gathered at Jacksonborough in January and February, 1782, threatening confiscation and banishment to all those who would not make some overt stand on behalf of the new state. Some were drawn out and did not suffer; others who remained at Goose Creek and in town did. When the law was passed, several categories were established consisting of those who had offered congratulations, those who had accepted commissions in the loyal militia, those who had been generally obnoxious, and so on. This action promised to bring about a complete overturn of property. Commissioners of the sequestered estates began to manage them, supplying slaves for public works and food for the army.

December 14, 1782, was the great day of deliverance. The Continental army moved slowly into town, while the British filed off to Gadsden's wharf. At three o'clock General Nathanael Greene conducted Governor John Mathews and the Council to Broad Street whence "every one went where they pleased; some in viewing the town, others in visiting their friends." Upwards of three hundred sail of the enemy fleet lay at anchor in the harbor, soon to depart. The townspeople, however, greeted the victorious Americans with cries of "God bless you, gentlemen! you are welcome home, gentlemen!"

The great dispersal of slaves and Tories took place with the departure of the fleet. Some of the slaves were taken to St. Augustine, some to New York and Halifax, and others to England. Very few of these slaves were ever recovered by their owners. Many, during the turmoil of the last few days, were also undoubtedly spirited away to

49

the backcountry by officers from that region who wished to stock their lands.

Although the loyalists were dispersed in even more directions than the slaves, many of them made their way back to Carolina. But when they appeared upon vessels in Charleston harbor, they were often forced, if under sentence of banishment, to wait many months before being permitted to land. Others had to return to England or at least sojourn in the Bahamas or in Georgia for a while until permitted to reappear in Charleston. Many never returned, but put in claims against the British government for property lost and received a proportional payment.

While this great dispersal of slaves and Tories was taking place, the patriots were swarming home. Many of the men at St. Augustine had been permitted by the British to move to Philadelphia, whence they sailed home or made their way home overland in the spring of 1783. After East Florida was returned to Spain by the treaty of 1783, the English there moved in large numbers to Charleston. Dr. Andrew Turnbull and Elihu Hall Bay brought their families from East and West Florida respectively. The devastation of war had created a great demand for goods and a vacuum among the mercantile community of Charleston, and enterprising men once again came out from England to make a fortune as their predecessors had done after 1748 and after 1763. As these groups tried to readjust during that turbulent year of 1783, there were many almost pitched battles between factions. Tories were dragged to the water pumps and doused. New men insulted such patriarchs as John Rutledge. Because of this turmoil it was found necessary, in the fall of 1783, to incorporate the city. The name of the city was changed from Charles Town to Charleston at that time. An intendant and thirteen wardens would compose the city Council, which would henceforth be the governing body of the city. Anyone who paid a three-shilling tax could vote, a requirement that was high enough to be protested. The intendant and the wardens were given strong powers for preserving order. They also took over all the powers that before the Revolution had belonged to the commissioners of the streets, of the workhouse, of the markets, and of the poor—as well as the duties of the packers and wood measurers.

The situation in the city was exacerbated by the attempt of the British merchants, led by John Nutt and Greenwood and Higginson, to recover monies lent before the war. Their right to do so had been guaranteed by the treaty of peace. This problem had been compounded by the great depreciation of money during the war. Some Charlestonians had been paid off locally during the war in depreciated currency. When many borrowed money to put newly acquired lands into operation, and the crops failed the two ensuing years, they too found themselves pressed by the agents of British merchants. Even General Nathanael Greene and General Anthony Wayne were pursued. When the legislature made it easier for men banished to return and to recover some of their confiscated properties, resentment welled up against the British merchants and their local allies. A growing conservative class found itself at odds with a more radical element among the people who were opposed to moderation, courts, and an elite. When it was discovered that the former officers of the Continental army were setting up a Society of the Cincinnati, the resentment was difficult to control.

What were desperately needed in the 1780's were new

lines of commerce, new sources of supply, to revive the economic position of the port and thereby bring back contentment among the citizens. But Charleston, once inside the British imperial system, now found herself outside it. The British, by an Order in Council in June, 1783, barred Americans from trading with the British West Indies. In spite of this discrimination, the Charlestonians depended upon Britain for capital, goods, and know-how. There was a tension between the need for the British and the hatred of them.

The reorganized Chamber of Commerce tried to extricate the city from this dependence. The four prewar officers of this organization had taken the King's side, but the new officers represented the patriot side of the mercantile community. When news arrived that American vessels had been taken by the Barbary pirates at the entrance to the Mediterranean, the British were suspected of having urged on the pirates. Thus, the Chamber tried to open up trade with France and Holland. Thomas Jefferson lent his assistance in the first instance, and Alexander Gillon in the second, but these efforts were never successful.

There had now grown up in Charleston for the first time a divergence between the patriot merchants and the British merchants. The fact that so many of the postwar merchants had British connections did something to tarnish the reputation of the mercantile community, which never regained the standing that it had had before the war. When the native merchants became less important, and the British were succeeded by the Yankee merchants after 1808, the commercial community of Charleston was looked upon as not entirely loyal. After 1790 the planters began to look down upon those in trade. Eventually the city was dominated by the resident planters, not the working merchants.

Although the new United States Constitution that went into effect in 1789 strengthened the commercial forces in the country, boom conditions did not return until after the outbreak of war in Europe between England and France on February 1, 1793. This war opened up the possibility that America might supply both sides with raw materials and foodstuffs. Could the United States remain neutral and profit from the distress of Europe?

There were arguments in favor of supporting France. In Charleston the planters, the mechanics, and a great part of the merchants had been ardent patriots. They romantically sympathized with France and her cause of liberty which, at first glance, seemed to be America's cause over again. But propertied men had second thoughts when they considered the possibilities of subversion. The arrival in Charleston of Edmond Genêt, the French minister to the United States, the forming of Republican Societies, and the plotting of expeditions against Spanish Florida and Louisiana were ominous signs. When the refugees from the slave revolt in Santo Domingo arrived in Charleston, these doubts were strengthened.

There were arguments against England: she was the recent enemy; she had prevented the new nation from trading with the West Indies; she refused to pay for the stolen slaves. Yet there were strong tugs in the British direction for she possessed the capital and the know-how, and she had many friends among the Charleston commercial community. What became the final and perhaps irresistible lure for the propertied classes was the fact that she had stability —an ordered society—something the local elite had always striven to achieve and greatly admired in others.

Yet there was the indirect trade with France and the French West Indies—the golden harvest of this war. France was unable to bring home her products from the West Indies and therefore opened this trade to neutrals, principally to the United States. The British, laying down the rule that trade not open in time of peace could not be considered open in time of war, seized many of the American vessels in the West Indies. She was willing, however, to let the Americans trade with the French West Indies by means of "a broken voyage." French sugar was brought to American ports and then transshipped to France. In return came French goods for the French West Indies. The value of this trade quickly rose, and Charleston had an unusual windfall.

By means of the Jay and Pinckney treaties with England and Spain of 1795 and that of Mortefontaine with France in 1800, the United States steered a middle course, trading with both sides and biding her time. Meanwhile, her commercial interests again grew rich. Much wealth was accumulated in the years from 1793 to 1808, the last great wealth to be gained by Charlestonians in the carrying trade. Nathaniel Russell, William Blacklock, Josiah Smith, Thomas Radcliffe, and Adam Tunno amassed fortunes which they displayed in handsome new houses.

Throughout the years from 1730 to 1808 the history of Charleston was that of the new America where opportunity was ever plentiful. Three generations had produced fortunes. Yet there was a tendency in Charleston for something different to develop. Her climate, her brand of politics, and her labor system set her apart. Yet until 1808 the ferment in the city was essentially American, with new opportunities constantly beckoning. It was only after 1808 that forces began to work which set her apart and made her, in the end, unique.

54

III.

The Sensuous City

ALTHOUGH CHARLESTON'S SOCIETY was continually disrupted, there was continuity. This continuity in the city's life came as much from the physical setting as from the generations of Charlestonians. The people came and went, prospered and went bankrupt; the rivers, beaches, and islands, the marshes, trees, and buildings remained, creating the sights and sounds, the taste, feel, and smell which lingered on for new generations to absorb, savor, and love. It is these sensuous aspects that make the city a tourist spot today, rather than the historical events that happened there —unless the events can be said to have left a glamor that enhances the senses.

A 1739 "Prospect of Charles-Town," published June 9 by act of Parliament, provides a picture of the city at the commencement of its greatest century. As the engravers noted, this was the capital of "the fairest and most fruitfull Province belonging to Great Britain." George Hunter's "Ichnography of Charles-Town at High Water," also produced in 1739, gives the location of each building, making it possible to describe the town in its entirety.

Bay Street paralleled Cooper River, its eastern side forming the curtain line that connected Granville's Bastion with Craven's Bastion. The western side of Bay Street was lined with buildings, stores below and residences above, most of them in an English style of architecture, but some with Dutch gables, a waterfront scene reminiscent of many of the old Hanse towns of northern Europe, or, because of the ambience of sun and sea, even of Cádiz. Eight wharves, or "bridges," as they were called locally, extended into the river. From north to south they were Crokatt's Bridge, Rhett's Bridge, Middle Bridge, Elliott's Bridge, Motte's Bridge, Pinckney's Bridge, Lloyd's Bridge, and Brewton's Bridge. Middle Bridge was the largest, and on it were grouped stores and the Old Market. A few imposing buildings broke the skyline. In the center, behind the Half Moon Bastion, was the Council chamber with the Guard House below; centered in the lower half was the Court House with the Exchange below; centered in the upper half was the Customs House with the secretary's office just beyond. Governor's Bridge extended Bay Street north to Colleton Square. Three principal streets led into the town from the Bay: Tradd Street from the Court House, Broad Street from the Council chamber, and Queen Street (formerly Dock Street, but recently renamed to honor Caroline of Anspach) from between Crokatt's Bridge and the Customs House. The Dock Street Theater was a block and a half west on Queen Street.

The first principal cross street parallel to Bay Street was Church Street, on which stood the most imposing building in the city, St. Philip's Church, built with funds obtained from duties on rum, brandy, and Negroes. This was the Established Church, its steeple the city's landmark. The French church and the Anabaptist church were also on Church Street. The next cross street was Meeting House Street, where the western wall of the fortified city had stood between Carteret's Bastion on the north and Colleton's on the south until demolished after the defeat of the Yemasees in 1717. The Congregationalists had one meeting house, the Scots-Presbyterians another, the latter recently built near the site of Colleton's Bastion. On King Street, just above Broad, was the Quaker meeting house and, just below Broad, was the Printing House, the home of Peter Timothy's *South-Carolina Gazette*.

Three new areas of town were opened up in the 1740's as the city spread well beyond the bounds of the walled city. In 1742 the Isaac Mazyck lands, west of what is now Legaré Street and between Broad and Beaufain streets, were offered for sale. The most noted feature of this section was the Work House where the Negroes were confined after they had attempted to run away or if they were to be punished.

In 1746, Ansonborough was laid out north of Colonel William Rhett's house, which had been built in 1717 on rising ground just north of the creek that flowed into the Cooper River beneath the ramparts of Craven's Bastion. This land had become the property of Captain George Anson, a British naval officer on the South Carolina station from 1724 to 1735. He first commanded the *Scarborough* and later the *Squirrel*, protecting the port from the incursions of pirates and Spanish *guarda-costas*. Between 1740 and 1744, Anson had circumnavigated the globe, commanding from the *Centurion* a small group of ships which swept the Spaniards from the Pacific. After a notable victory over the Spaniards off Cape Finisterre in the spring of 1747, which netted £300,000 sterling, he was created Baron Anson. Five streets were laid out in this new suburb: George and Anson, at right angles to each other, honored the admiral himself, while Centurion (now Society), Scarborough (now part of Anson), and Squirrel (now part of Meeting) were named after Anson's ships.

Church Street had been extended southward by a bridge over Vanderhorst Creek to Broughton's Battery, situated on Oyster Point. George Eveleigh's house, built on the extended section of Church Street in 1743, is a sturdy and handsome building of small, hard, imported brick with an interior finished in cypress from the low country swamps.

The construction of two buildings in the 1750's provided a formal center in a new style for this bustling metropolis. After the new parish of St. Michael's, named after a Barbadian parish, was cut off from St. Philip's in 1751, a church was built on the southeast corner of Broad and Meeting. There in the 1750's, under the direction of Samuel Cardy, was erected a graceful building in the Wren-Palladian style, its steeple rivaling that of St. Philip's as a landmark for the surrounding area. On the northwest corner of Broad and Meeting, in 1752, the cornerstone of the new State House was laid. The celebration on that occasion was held at the home of Alexander Gordon, who may have been its designer. Both of these buildings were completed by 1760. Between 1767 and 1769, William Rigby Naylor, son-in-law of Samuel Cardy, built a new Watch House on the southwest corner. The northeast corner was the site of the Beef Market, with a Market House built just prior to 1739. This new city center was just to the east of the point where Sir Nathaniel Johnson's covered Half Moon Battery (with its moat and two drawbridges) had stood. In 1770, the statue of William Pitt, commissioned by the South Carolina Assembly as a grateful gesture after the repeal of the Stamp Act, was set up in the crossway.

With the outbreak of the Great War for the Empire, there was a renewed interest in the fortifications of the city. An engineer, William Gerard de Brahm, who had come out to Carolina in 1751 with some Germans destined for Bethany, Georgia, was employed by Governor Glen to join Granville's Bastion to Broughton's Battery by building ramparts between, which would then be continued along the Ashley River. De Brahm carefully raised these ramparts four feet above the high-water mark which had been observed after the hurricane of September 15, 1752. Colonel Othniel Beale, "a gentleman of great ingeniousity and judgement," solved the problem involved in carrying these heavy works over boggy marshes under which no firm foundation was obtainable. Cedar posts were driven into the mud, upon which a cypress raft was built, which, in turn, was covered with earth. These mud sills were completed in ten months by three hundred men. The bastion between Granville's and Broughton's was named Lyttelton's in 1757 after the new governor. By 1775 the property owners on the Ashley side had leveled their ramparts and filled in the area behind at great expense.

De Brahm later turned his attention to a landward-side curtain line. The land north of what is now Calhoun Street belonged to Joseph Wragg, the most prominent of the early slave merchants. At Joseph's death in 1751 his lands were divided among his children. In 1758 his eldest son John sold 8¾ acres east of the highway leading out of town to the commissioners of fortifications, while Peter Manigault, who had married Elizabeth Wragg in 1755, sold 6¼ acres on the west side. A new curtain line of horn work, made of tabby (lime, sand, and oyster shell), was built across the Neck and fitted with a new town gate. In 1769, Boundary Street (now Calhoun Street) was laid off just south of this curtain line, which was the main line of defense at the time of the Revolution.

In the 1760's two of the leading merchants and Revolutionary patriots laid out suburbs northeast of Ansonborough, yet still south of the new curtain line. Henry Laurens created Laurens Square and, in 1763, built on the eastern edge of the square "a large, elegant brick house of sixty feet by thirty-eight," with piazzas on the south and east sides overlooking the marshes and harbor. Christopher Gadsden, who had acquired land just north of Laurens, developed it also in a suburban fashion. The principal new feature was a long wharf, the largest of the day, which bordered the Cooper River. The names of the streets in Gadsden's development, Wilkes, Pitt, Paoli, Hand in Hand Corner, So Be It Entry, reflected Gadsden's revolutionary fervor. Wilkes Street was named after John Wilkes of the famous Middlesex election controversy, Gadsden's suburb itself being known as Middlesex. Paoli and Hand in Hand Corner honored Paoli, the Corsican hero, who, after succumbing to the pressure of French power, had fled to England. "Hand in Hand" was the patriotic song of the Corsicans. So Be It Entry was named in defiance of the British.

The town was, at the same time, spreading on its southwestern and northwestern fringes. In 1767 the old Orange Garden just west of King, between Broad and Tradd, was carved up into lots along a new street named Orange, the development of Alexander Petrie. John Stuart built a fine home at the south end; James Laurens, Petrie's brother-in-law, another at the north end, which later became Edward Rutledge's. At the same time William Gibbes and Edward Blake were filling in the southwestern corner of the city and preparing to build mansions.

Harleston Village was the largest development, being approved by an act of the Assembly in 1770 and surveyed and laid out by William Rigby Naylor. This part of Charleston is now bounded by present-day Beaufain, Calhoun, Coming, and Barré streets. The street names in Harleston Village were, like those in Gadsden's Middlesex, taken from celebrated figures, both colonial and British, who were true to the Patriot cause. Beaufain was named after Hector Berenger de Beaufain, the late and long-beloved collector of the customs; Wentworth, after Lord Rockingham, who had been responsible for the repeal of the Stamp Act; Montagu, for Governor Lord Charles Greville Montagu; Bull, for Lieutenant-Governor William Bull; and Manigault, for Speaker of the Commons House of Assembly Peter Manigault. Manigault was later absorbed into Boundary Street as it was extended to the west. The north-south streets were Pitt, for William Pitt; Smith, for Benjamin Smith, late speaker of the Assembly; Rutledge, for John Rutledge; Lynch (now Ashley), for Thomas Lynch; and Gadsden, for Christopher Gadsden. The last three men had represented South Carolina in the Stamp Act Congress. Finally, there was Barré, for Isaac Barré, the Englishman who had spoken out so forcefully in behalf of the colonials.

This city-wide expansion was crowned by a magnificent building which was to dominate the waterfront. Over the Half Moon at the east end of Broad the new Exchange was built between 1767 and 1771, the construction of which was supervised by Peter and John Adam Horlbeck, who had arrived in Charleston in 1764. They went to England to secure their materials and undoubtedly their designs as well, for the Exchange is reminiscent of the new exchanges in Liverpool, Bristol, and London. The grand portico, with staircase sweeping up from the Bay, marked the formal entrance to the city from the sea. On these steps arriving dignitaries were met. Lord William Campbell, the last of the royal governors, was met here and, on this portico, the first goverors of the state were proclaimed, until the capital was removed to Columbia. George Washington mounted these steps in 1791 as he entered the city for the first and only time. More than anything else, however, the Exchange symbolized the aspirations of Charleston's commercial classes intent upon having a city as magnificent as any in England or in North America, a true seat of empire.

Although the site of the Half Moon Bastion and of the new Exchange had always been the formal seaward entry, the landward entry had shifted. Originally, it had been in the city wall just west of the intersection of Broad and Meeting. Then it had been moved to just north of Meeting and Pinckney, and thence to where King now crosses Calhoun. Thus King had superseded Meeting as the street that led out of town. Consequently, along King were grouped many small businesses which supplied the wagoners from the interior who brought deerskins down and carried goods back. It was the retail center, as Bay Street was the wholesale center.

Two areas just west of King had been kept open. One was the glebe lands of the Church of England with St. Philip's parsonage. The other area north of the glebe lands was the Free School lands, which had been bought in 1724 but had been taken over at the time of the arrival of the Royal troops in 1757, when wooden barracks had been erected on them. The barracks were used for the British Regulars until they were withdrawn in 1769. During the 1780 siege of Charleston the barracks were in an ideal location, just within the curtain line.

During the Revolution there was an attempt to protect the new suburbs by a ring of batteries surrounding the city, with improvements to the curtain line north of the city. Both Peter Henry Bruce and William Gerard de Brahm had suggested to Governor Glen that a ditch should be built across the Neck, thereby making the city an island. According to De Brahm, this provision would have secured the city from a sudden surprise from the sea, as well as against a Negro insurrection or an Indian war. In the first case, citizens could have sent their wives, children, and treasure into the country while they prepared the defense of the city. In the second case, planters might bring their families, effects, and provisions from the country to safety within the fortifications. Although a wet ditch was constructed in 1780, a canal to give the city some of the appeal of Venice was never dug.

Fortunately the Carolina patriots, unlike those of the French Revolution, did not indulge in a spate of name-changing after the Revolution. Charles Town did become Charleston, but King Street and Queen Street remained. Only Union Street, which had been named to celebrate the union of England and Scotland in 1707, suffered a change to State Street. Later, at the time of the adoption of the Constitution, the undeveloped parts of Gadsden's Middlesex became Federal Green.

New public buildings were erected in Charleston during the 1790's, made possible by the new commercial success. After the State House burned down in February, 1788, at the time when the capital was already destined for Columbia, it was rebuilt under the supervision of Judge William Drayton, an amateur architect, as the county and federal court house building. When, for a few years in the 1780's, it seemed as though tobacco would take the place of indigo as South Carolina's second crop, a public inspection system was established. Public warehouses to receive the tobacco from the backcountry were built in 1789, just east of King Street above the old fortifications, which area itself was to become Marion Square. Harmony Hall arose on the north side of Boundary Street, just east of Meeting, while the Orphan House was built in 1792 on the north side of Boundary, west of King. Gabriel Manigault, who had brought back from England a handsome library of architectural works, designed the Orphan House chapel. After the Market House, on the corner of Broad and Meeting, burned down in 1796, a portion of the market was sold to the first United States Bank, where, in 1800, arose a branch office building constructed according to the plans of Manigault. This magnificent building was to become the city hall. Manigault also designed, in 1804, a hall for the South Carolina Society.

During the war of 1812 a new line of fortifications was built across the Neck, along what is now Line Street. This pushing of the fortifications up the Neck indicates that the city had grown since the Revolution as new suburbs had been laid out. The villages of Newmarket and Washington, each of which had grown up around a racecourse, were still outside the lines, but Hampstead, laid out by Henry Laurens in 1769, was just within. Daniel Cannon had acquired land for two lumber mills just north of Harleston Village, which he developed after the Revolution as Cannonsborough and joined to the city by Cannon's Bridge. Radcliffeborough, in the center, was surveyed in 1786 for Thomas Radcliffe. John Wragg created Wraggsborough on the land he had not sold to the commissioners of fortifications. He laid out two malls on the east side of Meeting

Street. On the east was Mazyckborough, surveyed in 1786 for Alexander Mazyck.

In these boroughs some lots were larger, the houses often more spacious with copious piazzas, something of a cross between a townhouse and a country house. Many were built by planters as summer homes. In 1815 an Episcopal church, St. Paul's, was built in Radcliffeborough to provide for the new homeowners. This was often referred to as "the planters' church." There was, henceforth, until the Civil War, a division in the city between the planters of this part of the town and the merchants, who lived more generally in what was the old walled town near the docks.

After Jonathan Lucas had taught the Carolinians how to build rice mills, Cannon's, West Point, Toale's, and Chisholm's mills were built on tongues of land that extended into the Ashley, their mill ponds behind them. Bennett's mill was on the Cooper. Late in the nineteenth century and in the twentieth, these ponds were filled in. The Charleston Museum stands on the site of one, Beauregard Park on another. Colonial Lake was left as a pond. The one attempt to build a factory in these early days was made at the west end of Wentworth on the site of a battery, constructed as part of the revolutionary defenses, but that factory did not succeed.

Today all the creeks and ponds that cut through Charleston have been filled in, but where the creeks once flowed new buildings must be erected on piles. The present Market was built over one creek after 1804; Water Street replaced Vanderhorst Creek. At spring and fall tides these low-lying areas are the first to flood. Charleston's endless battle with the sea was fought in the eighteenth century by the commissioners of the fortifications who supervised the building of ramparts. Gradually the land was filled in behind. After Fort Sumter took over the major duty of defending the city, a row of palatial mansions was built behind the sea wall, which was raised to its present height in 1854 and afterwards called High Battery.

The Charleston single house and the Charleston double house became famous. The Charleston single house got its name from its one-room width. "The building stands with its gable-end to the street and consists, typically, of two rooms on a floor, with a hall between, containing the stair case, while a piazza runs along one side of the house (generally the south or west) to shelter it from the sun as well as to provide out-door living space. Entrance usually is through the piazza," which may present a false door to the street. This house was a practical solution to the problem of keeping cool and not an architect's house. When such houses were built in Harleston Village or in Radcliffeborough or in Hampstead, the porches became larger, but the basic form of the house was retained. It became the unique Charleston house.

The double house was English in form and design, although adapted to local conditions. The design was copied from an architect's book or modified by a gentleman architect or a master mason. What could be done quite early can be seen at Drayton Hall on the Ashley. But about 1790 most of the style known as Adam was introduced, probably by Gabriel Manigault, a style which soon flourished. Robert Mills, another native, began the Classical Revival with his pantheon-like Congregational Church, completed in 1806. The First Baptist Church (1819–22) and the Fireproof Building (1822–27) were later works. The Greek Revival,

66

represented by William Strickland's College of Charleston (1828–29) and Thomas Walter's Hibernian Hall (1839–40), also had some influence on domestic architecture.

The most intensive building of houses usually followed periods of commercial success or a great natural disaster. In the old city itself the oldest dwellings date from the 1740's, built after the great fire of 1740. The home of Robert Brewton, the powder receiver, and of Jacob Motte, the treasurer, stand beside each other on Church Street. The

West side of Church Street, Charleston
From a drawing by Alice Ravenel Huger Smith
COURTESY CAROLINA ART ASSOCIATION-GIBBES ART GALLERY

first is the oldest single house still standing, erected prior to 1733; the second was a double house, although the entrances are now at the sides. Both were barely missed by the fire of 1740.

The great mansion built in the 1740's was that of Charles Pinckney, which stood just north of the Governor's Bridge on Colleton Square, facing the Cooper River. This mansion, which contained over 300,000 Carolina-made bricks, was designed to emulate, if not excel, the finest mansions of that day. Since its kitchen and offices were in the basement, it stood up high, easily seen from the vessels anchored in the roadstead over the stores huddled together on the bridges and wharves. There was a curving entrance from Colleton Square, the house itself being reached by a high flight of stone steps. The open portico was faced with four white columns with Ionic capitals, surmounted by a triangular pediment of classical design, the roof itself being pierced by tall, solid chimneys. Inside, the entry hall was paved, as in Chief Justice Robert Wright's home; the best parlor was fitted with window seats, as in Captain Thomas Shubrick's dining room; and the second-floor rooms were wainscotted, as in lawyer James Graeme's home. Mrs. St. Julien Ravenel, in her life of Eliza Pinckney, wrote: "The whole house was wainscotted in the heaviest panelling, the windows and doors with deep projecting pediments and mouldings in the style of Chamberlayne. The mantel pieces were very high and narrow, with fronts carved in processions of shepherds and shepherdesses, cupids, etc., and had square frames in the panelling above, to be filled with pictures."

The finest Charleston homes were built to face the water

to impress the incoming visitor with the magnificence of
the city. Ironically, many of these early houses have been
hidden by newer homes built in front of them as the
marshes and creeks have been filled in. On the southwest
side of town William Gibbes built, just prior to the Revolution, a double house of large proportion overlooking his
wharf, which extended across the marsh into the Ashley
River. A double flight of stone steps led from a quay
to an entrance beautifully designed for the imposing
structure. In those days the house, constructed of the finest
timbers from the lowcountry, must have been, when
painted white, unusually impressive from a distance. Today
a new block of dwellings cuts off the view of the river.

The most exquisite home in every detail was built shortly
after 1765 on lower King Street by Miles Brewton, the
leading slave merchant of his day. This home cost £8,000
sterling. In *The Dwelling Houses of Charleston*, Alice R.
Huger Smith and D. E. Huger Smith have written: "It is a
square 'double house' on a high basement and is reached
from the street through a small courtyard paved with
flagstones. A fine iron fence with a double gateway sepa-
rates this from the street. The portico is very handsome
in its detail and the two tiers of stone pillars are impressive.
Its platform, paved with marble, is reached at each end by
two flights of marble steps with a broad landing at the
turn of each. Upon this platform opens the large street door
with its carved frame and fanlight. The wide flagged hall
has two large rooms on either side, and is prolonged at the
back so as to give additional room for the broad mahogany
staircase with a triple-arched window. Like other houses
of this date the drawing-rooms on the second floor take up

the whole front. The panelling, ceilings, cornices, mantelpieces, and other details are noticeably fine examples of the period."

When the Massachusetts gentleman Josiah Quincy dined with Miles Brewton in 1773, he was profoundly impressed: "The grandest hall I ever beheld, azure blue satin window curtains, rich blue paper with gilt, mashee borders, most elegant pictures, excessive grand and costly looking glasses. ... At Mr. Brewton's sideboard was very magnificent plate: a very exquisitely wrought Goblet, most excellent workmanship and singularly beautiful. A very fine bird kept familiarly playing over the room, under our chairs and the table, picking up the crumbs, etc., and perching on the window, sideboard and chairs: vastly pretty!" With its exterior design, interior furnishings, extensive servants' quarters, and landscaped garden, which at that time extended over several town lots, it was the most nearly perfect home in Charleston.

Of the great Charleston homes that now stand, more remain from the Federal period, 1793–1808, than from any other. The Charleston single house was slightly modified so that more elegance could be achieved from the simple plan. The entrance was placed on the northern side, which permitted a suite of rooms to grace the southern side. The Nathaniel Russell house, begun about 1808, was the masterpiece in this style. This transformation and the double house were the principal patterns, with each owner trying to outdo the others in interior decorations. The Joseph Manigault house, overlooking Wragg's mall, Thomas Pinckney's townhouse in George Street, the William Blacklock house at 18 Bull Street, Josiah Smith's at 7 Meeting Street, Colonel John Ashe's at 32 South Battery, the Simmons-Edwards house at 14 Legaré Street, and the Parker-Drayton house at 6 Gibbes Street are the chief examples of the houses built by this new commercial wealth. The tenement, known as Vanderhorst Row, at 78 East Bay, was also of this period. A tenement was a triple dwelling with the same outer walls and under one roof but divided by partition walls. Fortunately many of these fine homes, which were built in all parts of the city, have escaped the fires, although demolition has claimed a number of them, most notably Gabriel Manigault's on the southeast corner of Meeting and George streets and Thomas Radcliffe's on the northwest corner. The interiors of the latter, however, have been preserved in the remodeled Dock Street Theater.

The institution of slavery influenced the arrangements of the domestic buildings attached to the great houses. Slaves were brought into the city and sold "on the auction platform of the vendue master, at the race course between the heats of the races, in the public Negro yard . . . and at the wholesale warehouses of the big importing merchants." Even after the foreign slave trade ended in 1808, slaves were still bought and sold until the Civil War. In the city the slaves lived in the yards of their masters. This meant that each great house had a series of buildings extending to the rear. With so many slaves in attendance the kitchens could be at some distance from the dining room, usually in the next rearward building. In many instances the descendants of these slaves continued to live in the back quarters until the 1930's. Only in recent decades have the quarters and carriage houses been converted into apartments, and the city more completely segregated.

The interiors of the homes were magnificently executed, generally in the latest English style. Much of the ironwork

71

for fences, gates, lanterns, balconies, railings, and brackets may have been copied from *The Smith's Right Hand or a Complete Guide to the various Branches of all Sorts of Iron Work*, published in London in 1765, a copy of which is in the Charleston Library Society. The great gate and lanterns of the Miles Brewton house are excellent examples; the sword gate on Legaré Street the masterpiece. After the wooden balcony of a house in White Point gardens opposite Lyttelton's Battery fell in November, 1760, during a celebration of the King's birthday, after too many people had crowded upon it to watch the fireworks, there may have been a shift to iron balconies and therefore to a greater interest in ironwork.

The wood paneling, the mantels, and the plaster work required craftsmen of a high order. Mantels were brought out from England. Henry Laurens sold Charles Pinckney imported mantels for his mansion in 1747. The paneling and the plaster work required local carpenters and plasterers. The best examples of plaster work may have been done by William Purviss, who worked on the Radcliffe house before 1802.

The furnishings of these mansions can best be studied in the inventories. Benjamin Smith, who died in 1770, left a Broad Street home and a country estate at Accabee. The inventory records the furnishings of each room. His town-house drawing room contained one chimney glass, two sconce glasses in carved frames, ten mahogany chairs, and two carved mahogany elbow chairs, a card table, a tea table, brass furnishings for the hearth, and a small Wilton carpet. In a back parlor, which must have been a study and library combined, the furniture was also of mahogany: a backgammon table, two leather-bottomed chairs, a writing desk, and a bookcase containing seventy-three volumes, as well as two guns, one pike, one pair of pistols, and one broadsword. The dining room contained a Turkish carpet and seven family pictures interspersed among two sconce glasses, one pier glass, and one chimney glass. The dining table and the sideboard were again of mahogany.

Upstairs in the master bedroom were a mahogany bedstead, a red Morocco hair mattress, a feather bed, a chest of drawers, a night table, and a basin stand, as well as a wardrobe, a dressing table, a glass, and a carpet. The master's belongings included a gold-headed cane and a silver-mounted sword. In the coach house was a coach valued at £1,000, a chaise at £150, and a chair at £30, all no doubt made to facilitate the comings and goings between Broad Street and Accabee on the Ashley.

The furniture was either imported or derivative in design. Some came from England and from New England, but much was made in Charleston. The account book of Thomas Elfe, kept from 1768 to 1775, indicates that he made fifteen hundred pieces of furniture during that period. By 1740 there were a number of cabinetmakers in Charleston. Their numbers had doubled by 1750 and doubled again by 1760, increasing only gradually thereafter until the Revolution, which saw a falling off in numbers. In 1790 there was a spectacular increase to sixty-three, a number which mounted until the peak of eighty-one in 1810. After that the numbers gradually declined. Style was almost totally derivative. In 1756 James Reid advertised a house for sale in the "CHINESE" taste. In 1761, Peter Hall, a cabinetmaker just arrived from London, announced that he would make "for gentlemen and ladies of taste . . . Chinese tables of all sorts, shelves, trays, chimney-

73

pieces, baskets, &c. being at present the most elegant and admired fashion in London." Andrew Johnston possessed, in 1764, one Chinese cabinet with glass doors, "drawers under and Shakespeare's bust a top." The fact that the Chinese influence appeared in London during these years, indicates an almost instantaneous transfer of taste. After the war, although the vogue of Adam, Sheraton, and Hepplewhite still gave a strong English tone to furnishings, they were supplemented by furniture of French Directoire and Empire design. Charles Cotesworth Pinckney brought back French Directoire china and furniture.

The history of the silversmiths of Charleston paralleled that of the cabinetmakers. There were eight in Charleston in 1725, twenty-three in 1750, twenty-four in 1775, seventy-two in 1800, and only thirty-five by 1850, the peak of their output coming around 1800. In the eighteenth century, when there were no banks in the city, specie was transformed into plate, which sat shining upon many cupboards as a bold and visible sign of the new wealth. When reverses came, it could be melted down. There are few pre-Revolutionary silver pieces in Charleston; a fortune was carried off by the British when they evacuated the city in 1782. But what the silversmiths did make was beautiful in the eighteenth-century graceful manner.

The curtains and other cloth furnishings were equally rich. Governor Glen wrote in 1749 expressing his concern that the citizens of Charleston were importing considerable quantities of "Fine Flanders Lace, the Finest Dutch Linens, and French Cambricks, Chintz, Hyson Tea and other East India Goods, Silks, Gold and Silver Laces, etc." The inventories reveal the richness of these interior furnishings.

The history of painting in Charleston illustrates the increase in wealth. At first the artist was present by chance. Henrietta Johnston, in whose pastel portraits were first caught the faces of the planters and merchants, was the wife of Commissary Gideon Johnston. Mark Catesby, who drew birds for Sir Hans Sloan, eschewed portraits, but later Jeremiah Theus and Benjamin Wollaston tried to make a living by painting the portraits of the newly emerging rich. They did much to whet the appetite for more accomplished artists. Young Peter Manigault was discriminating in his desire to be painted by Allan Ramsay rather than by a less talented artist. Chief Justice Peter Leigh, on a trip to Boston in 1756, was painted by the young John Singleton Copley. Ralph Izard was painted by Zoffany; the Middletons, by Benjamin West; and both Izard and Henry Laurens, by Copley, the latter stopping for his portrait just after being released from the Tower of London in 1782. The emphasis was on preserving the human likeness, for there was little of the genre represented by George Roupell's painting in 1760 of a dinner party given by Peter Manigault.

The high period in portrait painting and in miniatures was in the 1790's, as it was in cabinet and silver making. The intent was that families were surely being founded for the new nation, and the founders wanted to be remembered. As Francis Kinloch said in 1788, when seeking a copy of the family coat of arms: "I would wish my Children to have all the Rights to rank, a distinction, which is to be claimed from Ancestry." By 1788 there were so many limners in the city that they formed a special group in the parade to Federal Green to celebrate the ratification of the Constitution.

John Trumbull, commissioned to paint a portrait of Washington for the city corporation, visited Charleston in

February, 1791. Rembrandt Peale, Raphael Peale, and James Earle painted most of the South Carolina Revolutionary heroes between 1794 and 1796. To these were added a host of emigrés from France and the French West Indies: Jean Claude Imbert, Monsieur Du Suaw, David Boudon, Monsieur Geslain, John Baptiste Rossetti, and Michael Samuel de Bruhl. Pre-eminent among the miniaturists was Charles Fevret de Saint-Mémin, whose wife had had estates in Santo Domingo.

Some sounds were constant throughout the period: the beating of the surf upon the shore, the wind in the trees, the calls of the birds in the air, the flapping of sail, the rubbing of rope, the lapping of water, the creak of wagons. But the babble of voices of the 1740's blended over the years into a Charleston accent partly shared by Negro and white. It was as though the city, like the mockingbird, was imitating all tongues. The Carolina mockingbird, with its breast and belly of light gray, wings brown and flecked with white, had an Indian name which meant four hundred tongues, for it was said to imitate all birds from the hummingbird to the eagle. The mockingbirds not only sang but, as Mark Catesby wrote, danced "by gradually raising themselves from the place where they stand, with their wings extended, and falling with their head down to the same place; then turning around, with their wings continuing spread, have many pretty antic gesticulations with their melody."

In 1706 the French Huguenots were permitted to use the French language in two of the established parishes. Until the 1740's the wills of most Frenchmen were in French, which would indicate that French was still commonly spoken, at least until the older generation had completely died out. The Scots who had flooded in lent their northern burr to the sounds of the city. As late as 1787 native members of a Charleston firm regretted that "in walking our streets, whether convinced by the Dialect or the Names of those who supply our wants . . . we should rather conceive ourselves in the Highlands of Scotland, than in an American state. . . ." From the 1740's to the early 1750's, when many "Palatine ships" came in, the number of Germans passing through the city was great. When James Reid advertised for three indented lads in 1750, he informed the public that they would be "easily known by their speaking broad of the county of Lancashire." Aaron Lopez wrote from Charleston in Portuguese. De Brahm had a Dutch accent. Occasionally there were Spaniards in town. There were Quakers with their thee's and thou's, and Indian dialects were heard when the Creek and Cherokee chiefs came to meet with the governors. Above all there were the sounds of the Negroes just off the boats from Africa.

Each accent was distinct among the original arrivals, but gradually two strains of accent emerged. In the two decades before the Revolution the young boys were sent to England for an education in ever increasing numbers. There they acquired an English accent of the eighteenth century, largely that taught by Thomas Sheridan, the father of the playwright. Francis Horner, the son of an Edinburgh merchant, wrote to his father from London in the mid-1790's: "With respect to one great object for which you were at the expense and trouble of placing me here, I think I am beginning to *pronounce* some *words* as Englishmen do, and just to *feel* the difference between the *rhythm* of their conversation and mine." Nearly a year later he wrote more

77

optimistically: "I am sensible that I have by no means made myself master of all the variety of the English accents: I am now and then detected in a Scottish inflexion, but hardly ever without previously detecting myself. This circumstance will inform you of the degree of advance I have made." The Charleston boys went through the same conditioning and brought home an accent with very special vowel sounds.

The Negro slaves, struggling to make themselves understood both among themselves and with their masters, who in the early days might be of either English or French-speaking stock, developed a language which combined African dialects with French and English words. The result was Gullah. No one knows the derivation. One school emphasizes the disintegration of English and French; the other, the retention of Africanisms. The first school claims that largely eighteenth-century English words were trapped in the Negro language and through mental indolence transformed. This indolence, according to John Bennett, "shows itself in the shortening of words, the elision of syllables, and modification of every difficult enunciation." The result is difficult to understand, "so great has been the sound-change and so complete the disintegration." Another historian of the language, Lorenzo Dow Turner, emphasizes the Africanisms. He finds much similarity between Gullah and Negro dialects of Brazil and the West Indies and finds the tie in the African origins. The real influence among the South Carolina Negroes came from the continual arrival until 1808 of Negroes fresh from Africa, for slaves generally came direct from Africa, not from the West Indies. Thus, over a one-hundred-year period, the low-country and the sea islands were crowded with Negroes.

What happened in the nineteenth century was that the aristocrats, by the time of nullification, had cut themselves off from the rest of the world and associated more and more closely with their native slave population; a bit of Gullah, therefore, found its way into the eighteenth-century English speech of the aristocrats, leaving a residue which is peculiarly Charlestonian—high Gullah, one might call it. It still persists in a few old families.

Tastes were as diverse in origin and as delightful in results as were sounds. The ingredients of the South Carolina diet came from the entire Atlantic and Mediterranean world: Jordan almonds, port, madeira, sherry, lemons and oranges from Spain, champagne, curaçao and grenadine syrups—benne seeds from Sierra Leone.

The way in which these ingredients were combined into dishes depended upon recipes handed down—perhaps from a French grandmother or a Santo Domingan grandmother or a German passing through Charleston or a lady from England—or brought home after diplomatic assignments in Europe, such as those of the Pinckneys in France or Spain. But, generally speaking, it was some combination of Old World culinary arts with New World staples. Real sophistication came from incorporating this international experience with the plain and local items of diet.

Each lady kept a book filled with recipes for dishes and nostrums. Eliza Lucas Pinckney's recipe book of 1756 showed already a high degree of sophistication. She had recipes for "Dutch blumange," "plumb marmalade," "orange flour ratifye," "mince pyes," "oyster soop," and "yam puding," as well as instructions about the best way to boil rice. These recipes were passed on to daughters, as Eliza did to her daughter, Harriott Horry, who began her

recipe book in 1770. But perhaps the best summation of
this art is to be found in the *Carolina Housewife*, written
by Sarah Rutledge and published in Charleston in 1847.
Sarah, born in 1782, had been taken to England by Thomas
Pinckney in 1792. Her brother was secretary to Charles
Cotesworth Pinckney in Paris, later in the decade. Undoubtedly they brought home the best of English, French,
and Spanish recipes, as well as those attributed in the *Carolina Housewife* to Italians and Germans. Among those attributed to Madame de Genlis were "potage a la Julienne,"
"smothered veal," "chickens a la Tartare," "sauce piquante,"
"green peas a la bourgeoise," "omelette soufflee," "coffee
cream," "almond ice," and "vanilla ice." But mainly the
recipes are of plain things well cooked, such as terrapin
soup, oyster soup, okra soup, and rice soup, or three ways
to make rice bread—Weenee rice bread, Ashley rice bread,
and Beaufort rice bread. The reader was told not only how
to dress palmetto cabbage, but also how to bake shad, to
dress turtle fins, to make shrimp pie, to stew crabs, to dress
oysters in cream, and to make caviar of mullet roe.

There were no short cuts in those days to preparing a
dish. All the good things took time, from the variety of
teacakes—apees, marguerites, jumbles, macaroons, mar-
velles, rusks, bunns, and wigs—to syllabub, Charlotte Russe,
blancmange, and Bavarian cream.

One recipe in full will show why a staff of servants
was necessary. This was Sarah Rutledge's recipe for turtle
soup: "Take the whole of the turtle out of the shell; cut
it in pieces, that it may be the more easily scalded. Throw
these pieces, with the fins, into the pot, and when scalded,
take off the coarse skin of the fins and lay them aside to
make another dish. The thick skin of the stomach must also

be taken off; under it lies the fat, or what is termed the citron. Thus prepared, it is ready for making the soup. Take a leg of beef, and boil it to a gravy, cut up the turtle in small pieces, throw them into the pot with the beef, and add as much water as will cover the whole about two inches. Let it boil slowly for about three hours. The seasoning and the citron should be put in when the soup is half done. To two quarts and a half of soup (which will fill a large tureen,) add half an ounce of mace, a desert-spoonful of allspice, a tea-spoonful of cloves, and salt and pepper, black and cayenne, to your taste. Tie up a bunch of parsley, thyme, and onions, and throw them into the soup while boiling; when nearly done, thicken with two table-spoonsful of flour. To give it a good color, take about a table-spoonful of brown sugar and burn it; when sufficiently burnt, add a wine-glass of water. Of this coloring, put about two table-spoonsful in the soup, and just before serving, throw in half a pint of Madeira wine."

The two important meals of the day were breakfast and three o'clock dinner. At breakfast there was always hominy with butter stirred in, eggs, bacon, leftover cold meat or cold shrimp ("one could have shrimp hot, with butter, but that seemed like winter supper"), and sliced tomatoes. The dinner at three was a tradition that began in the eighteenth century; it accorded with plantation hours and the tropical climate. It gave a long morning. As Anna Rutledge has written, "There was time and space; time for preparation . . . and space for storing."

The visitors to Charleston often commented on the food. In 1773 Josiah Quincy dined with Thomas Smith of Broad Street: ". . . decent and plenteous table of meats; the upper cloth removed, a compleat table of puddings, pies, tarts, custards, sweetmeats, oranges, macarones, etc., etc.,—profuse. Excellent wines." Quincy also dined with Miles Brewton: "A most elegant table, three courses, nick-nacks, jellies, preserves, sweetmeats, etc. After dinner, two sorts of nuts, almonds, raisins, three sorts of wines, apples, oranges, etc. By odds the richest wine I ever tasted."

There were many great occasions. In June, 1733, General Oglethorpe invited the Governor, Council, Assembly, and their ladies to a dinner, followed by a ball and cold supper in the Council chamber. The *Gazette* commented: "There was the greatest appearance of People of Fashion, that has been known upon such an Occasion." Banquets were usually given for the arriving governors in Shepherd's or Dillon's or Poinsett's, the most famous pre-Revolutionary taverns. To honor John Wilkes, a great celebration was held in 1769 at which forty-five lanterns were illuminated and forty-five toasts were drunk. In 1791, Washington was magnificently entertained at a great banquet held in the Exchange.

Perhaps the most elegant entertaining of public figures was in private homes. When General James Wilkinson arrived in 1809, Mrs. Thomas Radcliffe gave a ball in his honor at her new mansion on Meeting and George streets. Mrs. Gabriel Manigault left this description: "Genl. Wilkinson's band charmed us with some well executed military pieces—during which we paced up and down the spacious corridor which was brilliantly illuminated, & into her handsome bed room, which was likewise lighted. A variety of cakes, and wine, and fruit, and jellies, and all the nice things that could be collected were handed about. Everybody was in high spirits—they danced, and the band played during the intervals of dining—at eleven o'clock some delicious little oyster patties were brought up with other things of the same kind—after which the gentlemen were invited to partake of a supper of beefstakes and cold turkies—some of which was brought to the ladies—we retired at eleven but the party did not break up until two o'clock." Visitors who had tasted of these local delights never forgot them. Henry Laurens continued to supply the Earl of Albemarle with turtles after he acquired a taste for them on his expedition to Havana in 1762.

When spring came, the fragrance of the flowers hovered sweetly in the air; indeed, the smell of flowers was scarcely absent the whole year through. Mark Catesby, who had been sent out by Sir Hans Sloane, the founder of the British Museum, had first made Englishmen aware of the Carolina plants and trees. In his *Hortus Europae Americanus* of 1767 he described those that could be transplanted to England: the umbrella tree, the dogwood tree, the cassena, the live oak, and the yellow jessamine, which diffused its smell "to a great distance." He even thought the "Palmetto-tree of Carolina" might grow in England, for it was the only species of palm to grow outside of the tropics, and it flourished in Carolina. But there was none that could equal the laurel tree of Carolina, the magnolia grandiflora. As early as 1735, Sir John Colleton's estate at Exmouth, in Devonshire, had specimens of "this magnificent ever-green" adorning his garden. "Its ample and fragrant blossoms, the curious structure and beauty of its purple cones and pendent scarlet seeds, successively adorn and perfume the woods from May to October. . . ."

In one of the first issues of the *Gazette* in 1732, Charles Pinckney advertised garden seed from London. In this way the sweet alyssum, cornflower, daisy, foxglove, periwinkle,

83

snapdragon, stock, thrift, and violet arrived in the province. Nor were the West Indian flowers long in coming: the yellow begonia, the four o'clock, the lantana, and the parkinsonia. By 1730, Mrs. Lamboll had a "handsome flower and kitchen garden upon the English plan." Mrs. Martha Logan, of whom John Bartram said, "Her garden is her delight," not only sent seeds to England to Peter Collinson for the Royal Society but also at the age of seventy wrote *The Gardener's Kalendar*, published in 1779, the year of her death. According to David Ramsay, writing in 1809, this treatise regulated "the practice of gardens in and around Charleston" until his own day. Ramsay also informed his readers that Henry Laurens had a garden enriched "with everything useful and ornamental that Carolina produced or his extensive mercantile connections enabled him to procure from remote parts of the world." Laurens introduced "olives, capers, limes, ginger, guinea grass, the alpine strawberry, bearing nine months in the year, red raspberrys, blue grapes; and also directly from the south of France, apples, pears, and plums of fine kinds, and vines which bore abundantly of the choice white eating grapes called Chasselates blancs." Laurens was assisted by John Watson, "a complete English gardener," who later established the first nursery garden in South Carolina on a large lot stretching from King to Meeting, upon which now stands a large modern supermarket.

It was Robert Squibb who succeeded to the place of Mrs. Logan and of John Watson. He established a large garden on the south side of Tradd Street, between present-day Legare and Logan streets. There he experimented and, in 1787, brought out his *Gardener's Calendar*, the second publication on gardening in America. The gardeners were conspiring, as was almost everyone else, to make Charleston, by the 1790's, the most beautiful city in America.

A new firm advertised in December, 1786, "an extensive variety of the most rare and curious Bulbous Flowers, Roots & Seeds," such as "the most choice sorts of Hyacinths, double Jonquilles, Polyanthos, Narcissusses, Tarcetts, Tulips, double Tuberoses, Pasetouts, Carnations, with a great variety of Double Ranunculas & Anemonies, a sort of Rose Bushes, Etc." These items, "which have never appeared in this country before," had just been imported from Holland. In February, 1790, another firm advertised a great variety of seed and plants of flowering trees, lily roots, hyacinths, crowfeet, rosebushes, and potherbs which had just been imported from France. The Charleston Chamber of Commerce, calling upon Alexander Gillon and Thomas Jefferson, worked in the late 1780's to increase trade with Holland and France. These flowers were one happy result.

One of the unusual sources of new flowers was the East. The camellia was introduced into England from China by 1739, the mimosa from the Levant by 1745, the gardenia from China by 1754, the crepe myrtle from the East Indies by 1759, the tea olive from China by 1771, and the hydrangea from China by 1788. The man responsible for introducing the Eastern world influence to Charleston was André Michaux, a French botanist, sent by his own government in 1786 to establish a garden from which seeds of trees, shrubs, and plants could be sent back for the royal palaces. Michaux purchased land in 1786 about ten miles up the Neck near the road that led to Goose Creek between the plantations of the Cooper and Ashley rivers. This place became known as the French Botanic Garden, later simply the French Garden. From this point he traveled over the South and West, even going as far as the Illinois. He died in Madagascar on an exploring trip in 1802. It was he who introduced the camellia, the japonica, the ginkgo tree, and the candleberry tree. By following his advice, the surrounding planters turned their plantations into paradises. Although the gardenia was brought in before him by Dr. Alexander Garden at Otranto and the poinsettia was brought in after him by Poinsett, Michaux deserves first place among importers of new flowers. (The azalea and wisteria were introduced somewhat later in the nineteenth century.) It became a tradition for any visitor to Charleston to take the tour of the river plantations, for a spring day on the river was unforgettable. On Cooper River were Laurens' Mepkin and Middleton's Crowfield, on Goose Creek Garden's Otranto, Izard's The Elms, and Manigault's The Oaks, the last with its temples and bridges in the Chinese fashion. On Ashley River were Skieveling, Cedar Grove, and Newington, belonging to the Izards, as well as Middleton Place and Drayton Hall. The foreign travelers, from the Duke de la Rochefoucauld, to the Rev. Abiel Abbot, never missed this tour of country places.

The city markets were picturesque but full of smells. The oldest market had been on the Middle Bridge. The act of 1739 established a beef market at the corners of Meeting and Broad, where a new Market House had recently been built. It was open every weekday and remained at this spot until the Market House burned in 1796. In 1770, a fish market was set up at the foot of Queen Street on the Cooper River. By the time the city was incorporated in 1783, there were four city markets. In addition to those listed above, there was another at the western end of Broad

Street, where provisions and vegetables were brought from across Ashley River to be sold.

The markets drew the turkey buzzards, a constant and awesome sight in Charleston until recent days. Mark Catesby, in *The Natural History of Carolina, Florida, and the Bahama Islands*, has left an epic description of these creatures. Their custom was to roost upon tall dead pine or cypress trees; their food was carrion which they found by "a wonderful sagacity in smelling." On any day a Charlestonian might look into the sky and see what Catesby described: "They continue a long time on the wing, and with an easy swimming motion mount and fall, without any visible motion of their wings . . . no sooner there is a dead beast, but they are seen approaching from all quarters of the air, wheeling about, and gradually descending and drawing nigh their prey, till at length they fall upon it." A dead carcass would attract numbers, and, as Catesby observed, it was "pleasant to observe their contentions in feeding." They haunted the Charleston markets. When the Duke of Saxe-Weimar visited Charleston in 1826, the markets had been regrouped on the present site. "The market consists of five houses, in a long street ending upon the harbor . . . the most beautiful tropical fruit therein arranged, oranges from Florida, pistachios, and large excellent pine apples from Cuba. . . . Upon the roofs of the market houses sat a number of buzzards, who are supported by the offals. . . . They are not only suffered as very useful animals, but there is a fine of five dollars for the killing of one of these birds. A pair of these creatures were so tame that they crept about in the meat market among the feet of the buyers."

The presence of the buzzards and a certain smell were

proof that this was not entirely paradise. The waters run out of the harbor twice a day, leaving the mud flats uncovered, and, with a hot sun baking down upon decaying matter, there is an odor—not unlike that of Venice—to let one know that all the beauty is built upon unsure foundations. But the charm of the city is so great that even this smell is lovely to those who are born and reared in Charleston—it is the smell of home.

The Exchange (1767–1771).
Detail from Thomas Leitch's View
of Charles-Town, S.C., *painted in 1773.*

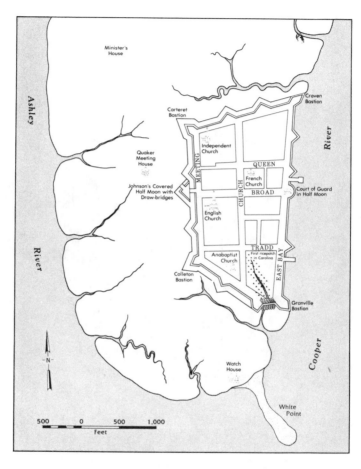

The fortified city.
Redrawing of 1704 map by J. Spencer Ulrey.

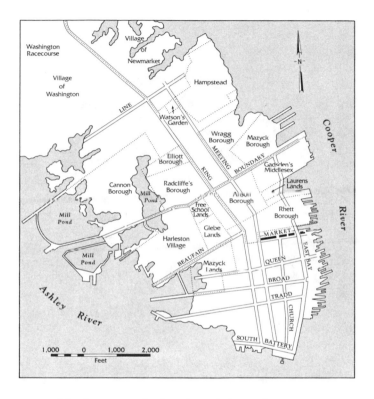

Charleston neck showing eighteenth-century
extensions (i.e., suburbs) of the city.
Redrawing of 1849 map by J. Spencer Ulrey.

A Charleston single house, No. 20 Montagu Street.

A Charleston double house, No. 64 South Battery.

Charles Pinckney (d. 1758).
Portrait painted ca. 1780 by Henry Benbridge
from an earlier likeness.

Charles Cotesworth Pinckney by Charles Fraser.

Thomas Pinckney by Charles Fraser.

Pinckney House after the fire of 1861.

Thomas Pinckney House,
No. 14 George Street, Charleston.

IV.

The Mind of the City

THE MIND OF A CITY is a product of the traditions of her people, of the education of her youth, of the reading and writing of her adults, and of the pleasures of her citizens. The principal traditions of Charlestonians were those of groups united by national origin or by profession. Prominent among the first were the French Huguenots. The history of their escape from France, both before and after the Revocation of the Edict of Nantes in 1685, was known to all their descendants. Indeed, the revolutionary tradition was a characteristic of all the national groups in Charleston.

The Scots were inheritors of the Presbyterian tradition of revolt against the Established Church of England. Even though the union of 1707 had removed the economic grievances, the religious differences still marked off Scotsmen from Englishmen. There was a second revolutionary tradition in Scotland, illustrated by the revolts of 1715 and 1745, the unsuccessful uprisings in behalf of the Stuarts. In Charleston most Scotsmen tried to dissociate themselves from those who had been defeated at Culloden by William Augustus, Duke of Cumberland. Governor James Glen and Councilor James Kinloch, both Scotsmen, spoke of the "unnatural Rebellion" in Scotland. On April 16, 1747, the first anniversary of the Battle of Culloden, all the gardens in Charleston were stripped of their "Sweet-Williams, which were worn by as many of the zealous well-wishers to the Protestant Cause and the Hanover Succession, as could get them." Although the wearing of sweet williams became an annual custom, Scottish merchants were always aware of an anti-Scottish feeling, which grew more intense after the ascendancy of John Stuart, Earl of Bute. But only John Stuart, the superintendent for Indian affairs in the southern colonies, felt the full force of this hostility, being driven out of the city on the eve of the Revolution.

Of the two revolutionary traditions which stemmed from Scotland, the one most important for the mind of the city was that which flowed through the dissenting elements in her society. The Rev. Alexander Hewat, who arrived in Charleston in 1763 to be minister to the Scots-Presbyterian Church, was always a foe of the Anglican church but loyal to the Hanoverians. His history of South Carolina, written in exile, for he took the side of the King, reflected his twofold position.

Among the professional groups, the clergy were strong channels of communication. The Anglican clergy should have set the tone of society, for they were of the Established Church, both in England and in South Carolina, and came to the colony fresh from their studies at Oxford and Cambridge. They were sent out by the Bishop of London, under whose diocesan care they served, or by the Society for the Propagation of the Gospel in Foreign Parts, answering requests from local vestries. Yet the dissenting ministers may have made more of a mark upon the local population.

Two of the commissaries of the Bishop of London did provide centers of intellectual life in South Carolina. Commissary Gideon Johnston, son of an Anglican clergyman in Ireland, helped to heal the wounds which had resulted from the clash among the dissenters, the Huguenots, and the Church of England men. He arrived after the establishment of the church in 1706 and worked diligently to embrace the Huguenots within the church and win the dissenters to an acceptance of the Anglican ritual. He was, according to Eugene Sirmans, an "able man, who soon learned the secret of dealing with Carolinians, which was to suggest rather than to command and to avoid any appearance of outside interference in the colony."

Commissary Alexander Garden was the chief antagonist of the Rev. George Whitefield in the first great intellectual duel in the colony. Although Garden was opposed to Whitefield's evangelical fervor, he was interested in uplifting the Negro race. Garden believed that each large plantation should have a Negro schoolmaster, a slave like those whom he taught, but one trained to read the Bible, to say the catechism by heart, and to use the Book of Common Prayer. He hoped to train some Negroes, who would then be sent out through the neighboring parishes to teach the other slaves. In 1740 the Society for the Propagation of the Gospel set aside 1,500 pounds so that Garden might purchase two slaves and open his school. The purchase of Harry and Andrew took place in 1742, and the schoolhouse was erected in 1743 on the glebe land near the parsonage house. Spelling books, Psalters, Bibles, and prayer books were sent over, and soon sixty scholars were at work. The school continued for over twenty years under the direction of the rector of St. Philip's, but Andrew died, and in 1768 it was necessary for the vestry of St. Philip's to send Harry to the madhouse. This early attempt at Negro education wrought no miracles.

After Garden, there was never another commissary appointed for South Carolina. For the two decades prior to the Revolution, the church was largely undirected in South Carolina. The pamphlets of the Rev. Thomas Bradbury Chandler and the Rev. Jacob Duché were reprinted in

Charleston on the eve of the Revolution, but these northern spokesmen had little support in southern Anglican circles. Their attempts to secure a bishop and maintain loyalty to the crown failed. With the Revolution, the high Anglicans left, and the church in South Carolina remained tinged with congregationalism.

The Congregationalists may have been more influential in pre-Revolutionary society than the Anglicans. The ministers of the Independent Church, Josiah Smith (1734–50), William Hutson (1756–61), and William Tennent (1772–77), were strong figures. Smith was the first native South Carolinian to graduate from Harvard, Hutson came out from England, and Tennent came down from Pennsylvania. Through them the English and American nonconformist spirit flowed into Charleston, a spirit which the members of the congregations, many of whom were New Englanders, shared. Josiah Smith spoke and wrote in defense of George Whitefield. Hutson, with the Rev. Richard Clarke, Garden's successor at St. Philip's, provided the leadership for a religious and philosophical society. And it was William Tennent who was principally responsible for the disestablishment of the Anglican church in 1778. From 1778 to 1790 the Protestant religion was established, but at the latter date the Jews and Catholics were granted the same legal rights to organize congregations as the Protestants had won in 1778.

The Rev. Oliver Hart, a Pennsylvanian who led the Charleston Baptists after 1750, was a courageous and tolerant man. He went on occasion to hear the Rev. Richard Clarke preach, and he invited the Rev. William Hutson into the pulpit of his church. On the eve of the Revolution, he and the Rev. William Tennent accompanied William

Henry Drayton on a journey to win the backcountrymen to the Patriot cause.

Since the Society of Friends had no ministers, each Quaker reflected the inner light. Sophia Wigington Hume, a child of the Charleston Quaker community, returned to Charleston from London in 1747 and again in 1767. After her first return visit, she wrote *An Exhortation to the Inhabitants of the Province of South-Carolina to bring Their Deeds to the Light of Christ, in their own Consciences,* which was published in Bristol and in London. Whether the Charlestonians responded to these pleas or not, the literature of the Friends abounded. The Charleston Library Society contained the classic works: George Fox's *Journals,* Robert Barclay's *Apology for the True Christian Divinity,* William Penn's *No Cross, No Crown,* William Sewel's *History of the Quakers,* and Joseph Besse's *The Sufferings of the Quakers,* the last work providing a detailed account of the persecutions of the Quakers in England and in America.

It would be incorrect, therefore, to think of Charleston as a completely Anglican enclave. Even though the Anglican church was established in 1706, the dissenting elements were strong in the city, although less so in the country parishes. Many members of the Anglican church were willing to think in congregational terms and sent their sons to academies conducted by dissenters in England. One Charlestonian wrote to his cousin, a Congregationalist minister in New England: "For my part I look on the difference [between the Anglicans and the Congregationalists as] of so little consequence that could I not conveniently communicate with the one I should with the other." In 1774 the Rev. William Tennent wrote his New England friend Ezra

Stiles that "the Episcopalians here are highly enraged at your Tory Clergy who are desirous of episcopal principalities, and many of the first in the province do declare to me that they will turn Dissenters in a Body if the parliament offers to send Bishops over."

The influence of the dissenters stemmed from the early policy of the proprietors who had sponsored toleration. Large groups of dissenters had come in the 1680's. In 1740 the dissenters were still over one-half the population, and the dissenting groups were always stronger in the city than in most of the lowcountry parishes. De Brahm wrote in 1772 that, although the city was divided into two parishes, there were six meeting houses, an Independent, a Presbyterian, a French, a German, and two Baptist, as well as Quaker and Jewish assemblages. Although the congregations differed in religious principles and "in the knowledge of salvation," there was no disorder, for the city since "its beginning [had been] renound for concord, compleasance, courteousness, and tenderness towards each other, and more so towards foreigners, without regard or respect of nation or religion."

The medical profession contributed the dynamic elements to the intellectual life of the city. To study medicine in the eighteenth century was generally the prelude to the study of natural history, for in the progressive schools at Leyden and Edinburgh there were formal courses in botany, chemistry, and anatomy. The students were particularly directed toward botany because of the predominance of vegetable remedies. After they returned from abroad, they kept up their contacts with the European medical centers while they engaged in the search for remedies. Here the medical profession's interest dovetailed with that of the gentlemen-planters who were searching for exotic plants for their gardens. By the middle of the eighteenth century there was, according to Brooke Hindle, "an international circle devoted to the cultivation of natural History," which was "one of the most dynamic intellectual forces in Europe and in America." From the days of Mark Catesby to André Michaux, South Carolinians corresponded with those in England, Holland, Sweden, Germany, and France who were interested in natural history.

In 1734 William Bull I was the first native-born American to receive a doctorate in medicine from Leyden University. Although he received a fine medical education as a pupil of Hermann Boerhaave, he did not practice upon his return to Charleston. Dr. John Lining, who was also a pupil of Boerhaave at Leyden, conducted experiments to establish the connection between weather conditions and diseases. His findings were published by the Royal Society of London. Dr. Lionel Chalmers of St. Andrews University, who worked closely with Dr. Lining, wrote *An Account of the Weather and Diseases of South Carolina*. Chalmers' chief work, *Essay on Fevers*, was published in Charleston in 1767, in London in 1768, and in Riga in 1773. Alexander Garden, a noted botanist trained in Aberdeen and Edinburgh, whose plantation, Otranto, at Goose Creek, was a botanical laboratory, corresponded with Cadwalader Colden of New York, Peter Collinson of London, and Carolus Linnaeus of Sweden.

The colonials missed libraries, publications, and conversations. This loss, they felt, could only be replaced by academies and societies modeled after those of England, particularly after the Royal Society of London. In the 1750's, while Carolinians were trying to remodel their Commons

House of Assembly after the English House of Commons, a few were also trying to reproduce some of the cultural models. When the Charleston Library Society was formed in 1748, one of its first acquisitions was Sprat's *History of the Royal Society*. In 1755 the Faculty of Physic was organized under the presidency of Dr. John Moultrie, but this was primarily for "the better Support of the Dignity, the Privileges, and Emoluments of their Humane Art." Lining and Garden conducted some electrical experiments, using Benjamin Franklin's *Experiments and Observations on Electricity*. Dr. Alexander Garden, who was himself a member of the Royal Society of London and who corresponded regularly with the Royal Society of Arts, tried unsuccessfully to stimulate the foundation of American societies similar to these groups. Clarke and Hutson's religious and philosophical group, formed at the end of the decade, was a successful conversational group. None of the Charlestonians passed into the great world as did Benjamin Franklin, but when the American Philosophical Society was formed in Philadelphia late in the 1760's, fifteen Carolinians became members.

Charleston made few contributions to "natural philosophy"—to chemistry, astronomy, or physics. Colin Maclaurin's popularization of Sir Isaac Newton's philosophical discoveries was in the library. There was interest in observing the transit of Venus in 1769, which was the great co-operative effort among colonial scientists, but bad weather intervened. The founding of the Charleston Museum on January 12, 1773, was an attempt to establish a center for the study of science. Peter Manigault's telescope was purchased for the museum, and plans were made to secure a Rittenhouse orrery, "the best concrete representation of Newton's mechanical world," but these efforts were interrupted by the Revolution.

The acquisition of Florida supplied not only security but also some intellectual stimulation for Charleston, for surveying often led to botanizing. William Gerard De Brahm, who was appointed surveyor-general for the southern colonies, and Bernard Romans, who first assisted De Brahm and then succeeded him, studied the geography and hydrography of the Floridas. De Brahm's *Atlantic Pilot,* which appeared in 1772, was a helpful sailing guide. Romans, who visited Garden in 1773, published in 1775 *A Concise Natural History of East and West Florida.* These men paved the way for William Bartram, who produced such notable word and line pictures of this southern region that they stimulated the imagination of Coleridge.

Charleston herself had not, however, produced these talented individuals through her own educational system. Most had been educated elsewhere before coming to Charleston. This was not to say that the city had no schools. The December 12, 1712 School Act established a free school in Charleston and one in each of the parishes. The one in Charleston materialized, but only at Dorchester was there a flourishing school outside the city. The commissioners of the Free School were to purchase land and erect quarters for the master and students. In return for the use of the land and buildings the master was to teach twelve free scholars; the others would pay four pounds per annum. The master must be of the Church of England and able to understand Greek and Latin. If he had a number of students, he was to have an usher to assist him and a writing master to drill the boys in handwriting and in numbers. In 1724 the commissioners bought a tract of land from

Thomas Pinckney, henceforth known as the Free School lands. There, by 1728, a schoolhouse was built, but, by the mid-1740's, the school was in disorganization and, by 1748, the *Gazette* noted that the commissioners had not met for four years.

It was Hugh Anderson who reorganized the school. From 1749 to 1776 he rented a house and served as schoolmaster. From 1750, he had both a Latin usher and a writing master to help him. During the French and Indian War the Free School boys were organized into a military unit and spent much time drilling. Some elementary education was, therefore, provided, though it was for but a few and those the sons of the middle rank of society, and even they could be diverted. Alexander McGillivray, the half-blood Creek chief, did attribute his later success to the education received in this school.

There were private schools established by trusts, such as the Beresford and Ludlam funds, or by societies, such as the South Carolina Society and Friendly Society. The teachers of these schools were not of high status. They failed to make a mark upon the older generation and influenced the young only in that they drilled them in the rudiments of learning. There was no center of higher learning in Charleston. The seeds for a college were planted, in 1770, when Benjamin Smith left one thousand pounds to found a college, and in the following year, when John McKenzie left his seven-hundred-volume library to the proposed college, the books to be placed in the Charleston Library Society until they were needed.

The sons of the leading citizens were sent out of the province for their education. They were quite often sent to England at an early age, either to study with one of the returning Anglican clergymen or to attend one of the famous public schools of England, usually Westminster or Eton. On the eve of the Revolution, a great number of Charleston boys were in school in Philadelphia. Those who went to England generally stayed on to attend the universities or the Inns of Court or, in some cases, to serve apprenticeships with London merchants. In the decade before the Revolution, there were twice as many South Carolinians attending the Inns of Court as there were boys from all the other colonies combined.

When they returned to Charleston, the boys brought back things English, in a superficial sense—the manners, the accent, the clothes, the new styles of the day. Sometimes the fathers thought they brought back too much taste for luxury and for dissipation, and they began to send their younger sons to the more Puritan Geneva. The Puritan ethic, which Edmund Morgan has identified in the Revolutionary fathers, was present in the older generation of South Carolina leaders, but it was beginning to weaken as the 1770's opened. Josiah Quincy, on his visit to Charleston in 1773, noted the decline, which was partly a natural transformation as the society moved into generations of inherited wealth.

The center of the intellectual life of the city was the Charleston Library Society, which was organized in 1748 by seventeen citizens, hoping "to save their descendants from sinking into savagery." Carl Bridenbaugh, in his sketch of Carolina society, wrote: "That this group numbered nine merchants, two lawyers, a schoolmaster, a peruke-maker, a printer, a physician, and only two planters eloquently underscores the vital contribution of the city to the literary culture of the Low Country." Among the 128 members of the society by 1750, the merchants, doctors, and lawyers were even more prominent. These men met together, ordered books, and read them in their society's rooms. They were also the men who read the newspapers and magazines in the coffeehouses and taverns, and the men who owned private libraries, as the inventories of their estates attest.

An analysis of the 1770 catalogue of the Charleston Library Society collection indicates what they read. There were complete sets of the contemporary magazines, such as the *Annual Register, British Magazine, Critical Review, Gentleman's Magazine, London Magazine,* and *Monthly Review,* as well as of the earlier pace-setting periodicals, the *Tatler,* the *Rambler,* and the *Spectator.* If from no other place than from these, the Carolina gentleman would have acquired an eighteenth-century literary style, such as the merchant Henry Laurens did acquire.

The most appealing subject matter was the history of the English civil wars of the seventeenth century. There were Bishop Burnet's, Lord Clarendon's, and David Hume's histories of the Puritan revolution, as well as a life of Oliver Cromwell. There were also the large collections of seventeenth-century documentary material, edited by Rushworth, Thurloe, and Whitelocke, which may have been hard reading, but the *Trial of the Seven Bishops,* the *State Trials,* and Salmon's *Abridgement and Review of the State Trials* were more exciting and perhaps more widely read. Besides history, there were the classics of political philosophy, most notably the works of James Harrington and John Locke, and the indispensable, and most widely read of all, Algernon Sydney's *Discourses.*

In her book *The Eighteenth-Century Commonwealth-*

man, Caroline Robbins has identified those writers who kept alive the seventeenth-century tradition of dissent in the eighteenth. They are the same writers whom J. G. A. Pocock has labeled "neo-Harringtonians." It is remarkable how many of these writers are found in the society's catalogue for 1770. There were Trenchard and Gordon's *The Independent Whig*, in four volumes, and *Cato's Letters*. There was a complete set of *The Craftsman*, which contained some of Bolingbroke's early essays, as well as his *Letters on the Study and Use of History*. There were the Irishman Robert Molesworth, the English dissenting ministers Isaac Watts and Philip Doddridge, and the Scotsmen Andrew Fletcher of Saltoun, Francis Hutcheson, David Hume, Adam Smith, and William Robertson, as well as the sermons of the liberal Anglican clergy: Clarke, Hoadley, Middleton, Tillotson, and Whiston.

Among the works of the Continental writers the story of struggle and dissent also predominated. Books about France and by Frenchmen included Davila's *History of the Civil Wars of France, 1559 to 1598* and copies of Montesquieu, Voltaire, and Rousseau. The interest in Rousseau was sufficient in Charleston for the *Gazette* to print the rumor that Rousseau was embarked on the writing of a history of England. Rapin's *History of England*, which appears in an earlier list, was one of the most popular works in the province. Histories of revolutions in the Roman republics, in Geneva, Naples, and Genoa, and in Spain, Portugal, and Sweden were plentiful.

It is obvious what the Charlestonians learned from their reading. First of all, they came to see power as the dominion of men over men. Power was aggressive, with a continuous tendency to expand. Power fed naturally upon liberty.

From their reading they had numerous examples of this form of tyranny. A story they cherished was of Massianello, the Neapolitan fisherman, a dealer in fish and fruit and a lover of freedom, who opposed oppression in the kingdom of Naples. In 1647 he refused to pay the tax on a basket of fruit. The police seized him; the mob released him. With the mob he went to the tax office shouting: "Long live the king, but down with the bad government." In the turmoil that followed, he became governor of the city and was betrayed and murdered, a martyr to the cause of liberty. Such was the story they read in Midon's *History of Massianello, the Fisherman of Naples*. Massianello was an early Wilkes or Paoli.

England had withstood the assaults on liberty taking place on the Continent, for there was in her constitutional system a balance by which the three orders of society (royalty, nobility, and commons) checked each other. This was the kind of threefold division that Lord Shaftesbury and John Locke had incorporated in their Fundamental Constitutions for Carolina. This intended balance, broken by struggles over religion and paper money in the early years, was only reached in the 1740's and 1750's, but the growing unity in Carolina was, in turn, threatened by the corruption of the English government in the 1760's. Unconstitutional taxation, weakening of the judiciary, plural officeholding, standing armies in time of peace, mistreatment of Wilkes, were examples of a settled, fixed plan of a gluttonous ministry to undermine the liberty of those merchants and planters who had settled in South Carolina.

The Charlestonians were as well informed as their Boston brothers about the new political theories through the contacts of the dissenters, with their like-minded friends in Old and New England, and the doctors, with their scientific correspondents. Charlestonians were also accustomed to printing their thoughts. The first Charleston imprint was Robert Johnson's proclamation in 1731 that he was the new governor. The next year appeared the first newspaper, *South-Carolina Gazette*, which the Timothy family, with Benjamin Franklin's support, made an important colonial newspaper. Peter Timothy was one of the organizers of the Charleston Library Society and in 1749 reprinted some of *Cato's Letters* from the edition of 1748. John Tobler began his *Almanack* in 1748. In 1758, Robert Wells, who had opened a large bookshop in Charleston four years earlier, became the publisher of the *South-Carolina Weekly Gazette*, which continued, after 1764, as the *South-Carolina and American General Gazette* until 1781. In December, 1765, Charles Crouch, defying the restrictions of the Stamp Act, began a third Charleston newspaper, the *South Carolina Gazette and Country Journal*, which his wife continued after his death in 1772 until the Revolution. After 1768, Nicholas Langford, from his bookstore on the Bay, competed with Wells. In the fifteen years prior to the Revolution, the newspapers were open to the political controversies of the day. Gadsden's "Philopatrios" items came out in Timothy's sheet; Laurens' "Philolethes" in Wells's paper. These were followed by the pamphlets of the Laurens-Leigh controversy, Zubly's sermons, and Drayton's pieces. There was also the growing practice to reprint works that would be of interest in Charleston: John Dickinson's pamphlets, Philip Doddridge's educational tracts, and the works of Richard Price and Cesare Beccaria.

David Ramsay was the best representative of this revolutionary intellectual tradition; he also suffered most in the postwar period, when the intellectual stimulation began to dry up amid the search for pleasure and stability. Through an analysis of Ramsay's work and the pressures from which he suffered, one can see the Charleston mind in transition, from Revolution to nullification, from cosmopolitan outlook to a provincial one. Ramsay was born in Pennsylvania of Irish ancestry. He graduated in 1765 from Princeton, served as a tutor for two years in a Maryland family, and then studied medicine in Philadelphia under Benjamin Rush, whom he ever afterward greatly admired. After practicing a year in Maryland, he arrived in Charleston in 1773. Since his father had been an ordinary farmer, Ramsay was a self-made man, of which fact he was always proud. He believed that "the great bulk of those, who were the active instruments of carrying on the revolution, were self-made, industrious men." By 1778 his Charleston practice was bringing him one hundred dollars a day.

He was a very religious man, formally a member of the Congregational church. He was devoted to the ministers of this church in Charleston: William Tennent, William Hollinshead, and Isaac Stockton Keith. The clergy, Ramsay wrote, "carried the gospel into the remotest settlements, and made an honest use of the rewards and punishments of a future state to promote peace and order in the present."

What made him unique was that his medical and religious interests induced him to think in terms of ameliorating the conditions of society. His three marriages brought associations which strengthened this strain in him. His first marriage was to the daughter of a Charleston merchant and brought him a fortune. His second was to the daughter of John Witherspoon, president of Princeton and leader of the Presbyterians. But it was his third marriage, in 1787, to Martha Laurens that influenced him most. This marriage brought him closer to the English evangelical movement, for Martha had been a friend of the Countess of Huntingdon and had absorbed much of Wesleyan pietism.

After Ramsay's death in 1815, Robert Y. Hayne wrote a personal sketch of the man. Hayne made two points: "His philanthropy was not founded exclusively on feeling, sentiment, or reflection, but was the result of all three. This was the great spring of all his actions." These were the characteristics of a man of the enlightenment. But, Hayne added, "Want of judgment in the affairs of the world was the weak part of his character." This criticism revealed Ramsay's idealism.

Ramsay was so imbued with the importance of the American Revolution that he devoted the 1780's to writing a history of that struggle. In 1785 he published a two-volume work, *The History of the Revolution of South-Carolina, from a British Province to an Independent State*, and in 1789 the two-volume *The History of the American Revolution*. Both works presented his view of the coming of the Revolution.

According to Ramsay, the struggle began in seventeenth-century England. "At that eventful aera the line was first drawn between the privileges of subjects, and the prerogatives of sovereigns." While these spirited exertions were being made at home in behalf of the liberties of the people, "the English Colonies were settled, and chiefly with inhabitants of that class of people, which was most hostile to the claims of prerogative." Those who came were chiefly Protestants, who loved natural liberty and the right of private judgment. "A majority of them were of that class of men, who, in England, are called Dissenters." Ramsay noted too that the members of the Church of England who came to the colonies were "without bishops, and were strangers to those systems, which make religion an engine of state." With this statement he correctly de-emphasized the importance of the presence of the Established Church in colonial South Carolina.

Ramsay believed that this natural division grew greater with the passage of time and of generations. Affection had eroded with each successive generation. Although their books were small in size and few in number, "a great part of them consisted of those fashionable authors, who have defended the cause of liberty. Cato's letters, the Independent Whig, and such productions were common in one extreme of the Colonies, while in the other, histories of the Puritans kept alive the remembrance of the sufferings of their forefathers, and inspired a warm attachment, both to the civil and the religious rights of human nature."

In America, according to Ramsay, all had been of one rank. Each had a part of that earth which God had so generously bestowed upon them. Farmers were self-reliant and, because of moderate circumstances, deprived of all "superfluity for idleness, or effeminate indulgence." The people had not been subverted by high offices, which had been reserved for the natives of Britain. Nor had "the enervating opulence of Europe" reached the colonies. By the conquest of Canada, they had been released of all fears of hostile neighbors and thus stood more readily alone. And yet, until 1763, the colonists were content. Then there was a changed attitude toward England; instead of being an "affectionate Mother," she now seemed "an illiberal stepdame." Neither reason nor logic could settle the difference, for something like the contrariness of human nature was at work. As commonly happens in discussions of doubtful claims between states, the ground of the original dispute shifted. While the mind investigated one subject, other matters came into view. In opposing tyranny, liberty became better understood. Ramsay concluded: "Unfortunately for both countries, two opinions were generally believed, neither of which was perhaps true in its utmost extent, and one of which was most assuredly false. The Ministry and Parliament of England proceeded on the idea, that the claims of the Colonists amounted to absolute independence, and the fixed resolution to renounce the sovereignty of Great Britain was concealed under the specious pretext of a redress of grievances. The Americans, on the other hand, were equally confident that the Mother Country not only harboured designs unfriendly to their interests, but seriously intended to introduce arbitrary government. Jealousies of each other were reciprocally indulged to the destruction of all confidence, and to the final dismemberment of the empire."

Ramsay's work was notable not only because it presented a reasonable explanation of past events but also because it was suffused with hope for the new America. The last three pages of volume two of *The History of the American Revolution* were didactic in tone. He wanted his contemporaries to make the American Revolution an era "remarkable for the progressive increase of human happiness. . . . It is now your turn to figure on the face of the earth, and in the annals of the world." Later, when he wrote his biography of George Washington, he dedicated it to "Emperors, Kings, and others, exercising sovereign power in the old World; in hopes that from the example of George Washington in the New, they will learn to avoid War, to promote good will in the family of mankind, and use all the power they possess, for the Public Good." He saw the Revolution as releasing creative energy. In his famous Fourth of July oration in 1778, he had noted that "the Royal Society, the great nursemaid of science, in the colonies, had been founded 'immediately after the termination of the civil wars in England.' " He therefore looked for signs of new creativity in the arts and sciences and thought he saw it presaged in Jedidiah Morse's geography, David Bushnell's submarine, Benjamin Rush's cure for lockjaw, and Hamilton's series of letters signed "Publius." But this was where his own community began to let him down.

On May 1, 1787, Ramsay wrote to Benjamin Rush: "I am ashamed to tell that only three sets of the Philosophical transactions have sold in this state. . . . I long to see the day when an author will at least be on an equal footing with a taylor or shoemaker in getting his living." Of course, Ramsay wanted to be recognized as a great historian, and even to make money from his books, but this desire was never fulfilled. He was elected a member of the new Massachusetts Historical Society, but no such society flourished in Charleston. He was unsuccessful in his long term aims for the Santee Canal, of which company he was the president. Although it was constructed, it never developed the state, and it lost money. Above all, he met failure in the political arena, being defeated in 1788 for a seat in Congress from Charleston district, and in 1794 for a seat in the United States Senate. On both occasions his views on slavery undermined him. It was suspected that he was in favor of abolition. His life ended in tragedy. He was shot by a madman whom he had attempted to help.

In Charleston the Revolution was more disrupting than

fertilizing. Some of the leading intellectuals took the King's side: Alexander Garden principally, as well as Alexander Hewat and Robert Wells. Both the Charleston Library Society and the Charleston Museum had difficulty getting started again after the war. They had both suffered severe losses in the fire of 1778, which had destroyed six to seven thousand books, paintings, prints, a pair of elegant globes, and mathematical instruments. Even the attempt to found a college, revived in 1785, took a decade to succeed. The brick barracks on the old Free School lands were converted into classrooms and dormitories. Although the college opened in 1790 and the first class graduated in 1794, there were no notable professors until the nineteenth century. The Anglicans were as slow in securing a bishop. The Rev. Robert Smith, who had succeeded Richard Clarke in the pulpit of St. Philip's, had been a patriot, and in 1795, he was consecrated the first bishop of South Carolina. After he died in 1800, twelve years intervened before another bishop was consecrated. Yet, in the five years that he served, Smith did not create a center of intellect and strength as had Commissaries Johnston and Garden. There was, of course, in the 1780's, a need for almost everyone to recover his fortune, or to win one. When new wealth was achieved in the nineties, there was a difference in tone from the decade of the 1750's, which had also seen the growth of new wealth, the erection of public buildings, and the stimulation of the arts. In the 1790's, there was more of an emphasis on fashion than intellect, a striving for form rather than substance.

New modes of enjoyment were introduced. Although Andrew Johnston had brought his golf clubs from Scotland before the Revolution, the game of golf was not played until the decade after the Revolution. In 1786 the British merchants, largely Scottish, who had stayed on, formed a golfing society and played the game on Harleston Green.

Charleston had had a theater since 1735, when the Dock Street Theater first opened. Plays were given from time to time by traveling companies, and on occasion a play became a vehicle of reform. Joseph Addison's *Cato*, which was presented on a number of occasions, was a play which taught the viewer to be suspicious of tyranny. In 1773–74, 118 performances were given in Charleston, including eleven of Shakespeare's plays. It was the most brilliant dramatic season in colonial America.

The revival of interest in the theater in the 1790's elicited some protests from those who thought the theater was now a vehicle of reaction. In 1793 the Charleston Theater was built on Savage Green, facing Broad Street. The building was 125 feet long, 56 feet wide, and 37 feet high, with a large flight of stone steps and a palisaded courtyard. The stage was 56 feet long, "the front circular with three rows of patent lamps." The Charleston Theater opened on January 22, 1794, with a performance of *The Tragedy of the Earl of Essex*. In February there was a benefit performance for the refugees from Santo Domingo. This theater, which the Federalists attended, produced such plays as *King Richard III*, *Hamlet*, *Prince of Denmark*, and *The Life and Death of Mary Queen of Scots*.

The plays were considered aristocratic ones and drew the following letter from a pro-French Republican: "If on the American Stage we are to be entertained with dramatic productions exhibiting the theatrical foppery of passionate Kings, pouting Queens, rakish Princes, and flirting Princesses, Knavish Ministers and peevish Secretaries, lamenting misfortunes in which the bulk of mankind are no way concerned; daggering, poisoning, or hanging themselves for grievances that are purely imaginary, better we were without them. . . . It has ever been the policy of ministers of state, in all monarchical governments merging towards monarchy, to create and countenance alluring amusements in order to prevent the people from thinking. A few years ago when parties ran high in England, Garrick was employed by the Government to give a jubilee in honor of Shakespeare at Stratford-upon-Avon. The scheme succeeded beyond expectation: Wilkes and Liberty were neglected and for a long time nobody meddled with politics."

A rival theater, known as the French Theater or City Theater, was opened on April 10, 1794, on the west side of Church Street between St. Michael's Alley and Tradd Street, with a benefit performance for the American captives of the Algerines. The French Theater presented more "democratic" forms of amusement, harlequinades, clowns, and "a celebrated rope dancer." "The light, gay, fantastic offerings at the French Theatre, full of color, motion, and good music" caught the fancy of the Republicans.

Both theaters were filled for many months; they even remained open during the summer season, impossible as that might seem in Charleston's climate. In June, 1794, the Charleston Theater announced that it had installed an air pump like those used on prison ships in which four to six hundred prisoners were kept in the hold. Six days later the rival theater announced that it had "made an improvement on a Fan in the possession of a gentleman in Charleston, sufficiently calculated to form a pleasing coolness without the least inconvenience to any individual."

Throughout the decade they continued to compete, providing the town with entertainment as well as gossip, for the private lives of the players afforded a number of scandals. Alexander Placide, the celebrated rope dancer, was involved in several affairs. The noted Sully family cut a wide swath through Charleston society after Matthew Sully (whose sister was the wife of Thomas Wade West, manager of the Charleston Theater) brought his family to town. His daughter Julia married Belzon, the French miniaturist with whom his famous son Thomas had begun his artistic studies. Another daughter, Elizabeth, eloped with Middleton Smith.

The St. Cecilia Society, founded in 1735, had held concerts before the Revolution, but now with Thomas Pinckney sending instruments from England and many musically talented Santo Domingans arriving, the quality of performances was raised. In this decade Charleston had a symphony orchestra, two fine theater orchestras, a chorus for the opera, and excellent singers. The tradition of fine organ music at St. Philip's and St. Michael's was also continued. On December 17, 1793, the St. Cecilia Society held a concert at Williams' Coffee House, where it often met, for the benefit of newly arrived French musicians. On March 6, 1794, there was another concert for the distressed refugees from Santo Domingo. On these occasions the music of Haydn, Davaux, Corelli, Pleyel, and Gretrie was played. The public concerts were supplemented by musical evenings at home. In a letter to Thomas Pinckney in London, August 25, 1792, Charles Cotesworth Pinckney described a private concert at the home of Mrs. Middleton, who presided every Wednesday evening over her musical salon.

A change from interest in cockfighting to one in horse racing may be evidence of an improvement in taste, though not in intellectual stimulation. In the 1730's cockfighting was the rage, champion cocks being taken to any parish to meet a challenger. In May, 1735, the Port Royal Cocks won seven battles in eight over those of Christ Church parish "and a considerable Sum of Money was won and lost on the Diversion." In November, 1735, the owner of a "muffled cock, named Bougre de Sot" offered to let him fight any cock in the province.

Pride in cocks was superseded during the colonial period by a pride in horses. Thomas Nightingale opened the Newmarket Course in 1754 on Charleston Neck. By 1762 the pedigree of race horses seemed as important as that of families, if the following advertisement, which appeared in the *Gazette* on November 6, 1762, was a true sign:

"The high bred Horse Pharaoh will cover the ensuing season at Drayton-Hall, near Ashley-ferry, at Five Guineas each mare. And, for the satisfaction of gentlemen who chuse to send mares, the under-mentioned is his undoubted pedigree . . . which is more than can be said for any horse ever yet imported into this province.

"He was bred by Lord Gower, got by his own Stallion called Moses, and foaled 5th May 1753. His dam was got by Lord Godolphin's Arabian, out of his Mixbury mare, who was got by Darley's Arabian, out of Sr. Matthew Pearson's mare that was the dam of Terror; her grand dam by Lord Wharton's Old Snail; her great grand dam by Burford Ball, out of a mare of Mr. Williamson's. Ball was got by Brimmer, and his dam was a Dayton barb mare!—He is therefore full brother, on the mare's side to Brutus and Tarquin, they being got by sons of the Godolphin Arabian, and he out of a daughter of the said Arabian. . . . Those mares first engaged to be sent, shall be first served."

The most famous stable was the Johns Island stud owned by Edward Fenwick of Fenwick Hall. Fenwick took the Tory side during the Revolution and suffered the confiscation of his estate. Although he recovered a portion of his estate by special act of the legislature in 1785, he was still forced to sell his horses three years later. It was at the dispersal of this stable that many planters secured "high-bred" horses with which to found their own studs. These horses were soon racing at the new, more fashionable track, the Washington Racecourse, which was established just north of the village of Washington, the site of present-day Hampton Park. General Charles Cotesworth Pinckney, General William Washington, General William Moultrie, General Jacob Read, William Alston, O'Brien Smith, Gabriel Manigault, Wade Hampton, and Edward Fenwick had organized the fourth South Carolina Jockey Club in 1792, which organization was the owner of the racecourse. The first race on the new course was on February 15, 1793.

Race week in February became the most important week of the year for society. The planters and their families flocked to Charleston for a round of balls and parties. It was then that the punches were drunk, the delicious meals served, the new fashions worn. Elegant coaches with liveried servants rolled through the streets. The booths at the racecourse were gaily decorated. John Randolph of Roanoke, who visited Charleston in February, 1796, spoke of "the display of beautiful women, gallant fellows, and elegant equipages" as "unusually brilliant."

Had peace and affluence begun to sap the intellectual

vivacity of the citizenry? Was the pursuit of pleasure becoming a principal part of life? Certainly luxurious living was at its height in this decade. At the end of the decade, a pleasure garden, Vaux Hall, was opened on Friend (now Legaré) Street between Broad and Queen, not more than two blocks from the Charleston Theater:

> *Where the jet d'eau delights the eye,*
> *Throwing its waters to the sky,*
> *While Hail Columbia! from the band*
> *Proclaims a free and happy land.*

V.

The Pinckney Family

WHY DID CHARLESTON vote to join the Union in 1788? Why did she vote in 1860 to withdraw from the Union? In May, 1788, South Carolinians met in the City Hall, the State House having burned in February, and ratified the Constitution; in December, 1860, they met in Institute Hall on Meeting Street, not two blocks from the site of the old State House, and voted to secede. Since the same elite guided the destinies of the city and of the state from the Revolution to the Civil War, there must have been a change in thought in the intervening years concerning the value of the Union to this rice- and cotton-planting society. South Carolina voted for ratification in May, 1788, and Charleston and the neighboring parishes voted unanimously in favor of adopting the Constitution. The center of Federalist strength was, therefore, in the city. An analysis of the forces supporting the Federalist party will give an answer to the first question. The remainder of this book will provide an answer to the second.

William Loughton Smith, who represented Charleston District in the first five Congresses, was the most active of the Federalist politicians. He was supported by the British merchants who had stayed on after the Revolution; by the old Tories who had gradually won their way back into local society by having their friends remove their names from the lists of those who had been banished and whose estates had been confiscated; by the holders of the state debt, particularly those who had lent money to the state prior to 1780; by the new leaders of the Charleston Chamber of Commerce, who wanted protection for their vessels from the Barbary pirates and admission to the trade of the British West Indies; and by the directors of the Santee Canal Company, who were looking for English and Yankee capital to open up the backcountry. Smith fitted in perfectly with these interests. He was the son of Benjamin Smith, successful merchant and speaker of the Commons House of Assembly. His English education had continued throughout the war years under the supervision of John Nutt, whom he represented in the 1780's, in the collection of old debts. By his marriage to Charlotte Izard he became the son-in-law of Ralph Izard, a Goose Creek resident with vital interests in the Santee Canal Company, and of Alice DeLancey Izard, who had important New York connections. Through summering in the north, Smith knew personally most of the wealthy northerners. On one occasion, in 1790, when discussing the assumption of state debts, he wrote that "New England, New York, and I met." Smith, therefore, worked to secure the funding of the debt, the establishment of the United States Bank (Smith's friends becoming directors of the branch in Charleston), a pro-English commercial policy, and ratification of the Jay Treaty. But, by supporting such a program, Smith was a strange figure to lead an agrarian society, for that is what South Carolina has traditionally been considered.

An analysis of the entire South Carolina Federalist party might indicate that their support was somewhat wider than that represented in the figure of William Smith. It was a coalition of factions, somewhat like those factions described by Sir Lewis Namier as existing in pre-1776 England. Within Charleston there were, during the 1790's, four distinct Federalist factions. Ralph Izard, with his two sons-in-law, William Loughton Smith and Gabriel Manigault, composed the Izard-Manigault-Smith faction. Izard, a planter, had married his daughters to the son and grandson of prominent merchants. All three were large holders of the public debt. Izard was the first senator, and Smith the first representative. Josiah Smith, Jr., George Smith, Daniel De-Saussure, and Edward Darrell, who were partners in the one major patriotic mercantile establishment, Smiths, DeSaussure, and Darrell, were another. They were the leaders of the new Chamber of Commerce and directors of the branch bank. Jacob Read, whose father had owned a Charleston ropewalk, and James Simons, a relation of Read's by marriage, formed a third faction. Jacob Read succeeded Izard as senator; James Simons was naval officer of the port. The Pinckneys and the Rutledges were the fourth faction.

These Charleston factions were strongly supported by two planting factions, one centering around Georgetown and the other around Beaufort. Isaac Huger, and later his nephew Benjamin Huger, led the Georgetown rice planters; Robert Barnwell, the Beaufort rice planters.

This was leadership by an elite, for all these men were members of families established prior to the Revolution. These families had also provided the patriotic leadership during the American Revolution. They stood out because of their antecedents, their wealth, and the prestige gained from winning the recent struggle. Theirs was a government by men who felt no need to electioneer.

In South Carolina opposition to the aristocratic elite could come only from the lesser folk within the city or from the backcountry, particularly that part above the fall line. But since it was a deferential society, there was little chance for these groups to push forward their own leaders.

There were, of course, rumblings of discontent. Within the city, during the 1790's, many of the tradesmen banded together into the Republican Society of Charleston, greeted Genêt rapturously, and sympathized with the aims of the French Revolution, at least in its earliest stages. The excesses of the Revolution and Federalist scorn for the self-created Republican society withered the tradesmen's attempt to unite. From the backcountry came pressure for a removal of the capital from Charleston and more representation. Charles Cotesworth Pinckney led the battle which compromised these matters in the new state constitution of 1790. Columbia did become the capital, and more representation was granted, but the state offices were duplicated in Charleston. Still, in 1794, there were strong upcountry demands for further changes in representation. But an influence that was always at work was described in Aedanus Burke's famous letter setting forth the way in which the backcountry members of the ratification convention had been seduced by the good food and drink of the Charleston nabobs. By merely tipping their hats to upcountry acquaintances in town for race week, the imperious generals of the Jockey Club could hold many in line.

About the only type of person who could rise in opposition would be younger sons of families within the charmed circle, young men who were not given their places in the sun rapidly enough. If the younger men thought that they had special advantages which were not recognized (such as Pierce Butler's high rank in the Irish aristocracy or Charles Pinckney's exceptional mental talents), then they might be more vehement in their demands. The grand old men of the Jockey Club could not quite squelch them.

The classic battle was, therefore, the one that took place

within the old order—in fact, among members of the Pinckney family. No family more fully illustrates the economic, political, military, and constitutional history of Charleston during the golden century than does the Pinckney family. From the 1730's, when Charles Pinckney, as speaker of the Commons House of Assembly, championed the rights of that body against the claims of the royal authority, until the 1830's, when Henry Laurens Pinckney tried to gag the Congress of the United States, the Pinckneys were present at every major historical step in South Carolina's unfolding story.

The story of the Pinckneys begins with the brothers Charles (1699–1758) and William (1704–66), both of whom were born in Carolina, the sons of Thomas Pinckney and his wife, Mary Cotesworth, who had come from Durham in the north of England. Charles, a lawyer, represented the Charleston and London merchants in the local courts, thereby becoming intimately connected with the commercial rise of the city. He was first elected to the Assembly in the early 1730's. In time he became its speaker (1736–40), being the chief spokesman in defense of the privileges of that body at the time when it was asserting itself against the governor and the Council.

In 1744, after the death of his first wife, Charles Pinckney married Eliza Lucas, the daughter of the governor of Antigua, who owned a plantation just north of Wappoo Creek near the Stono River. There she had experimented with the culture of indigo, making a contribution to the colony's economic well-being, almost as important as her husband's contribution to the provincial political institutions. In 1745, as if to celebrate their joint success, they began to build, on Colleton Square, one of the great Charleston mansions, which they rented to Governor James Glen upon their departure for England. It was with great care that they also managed their estate of Belmont, five miles north of the city on the Neck. By 1752 the Pinckneys had a sizable rent roll.

Three children were born to them: Charles Cotesworth (1746), Harriott (1748), and Thomas (1750). With wealth and a family, the father began to think of securing for himself a high place in British society. It was quite fitting that he should be appointed a member of the royal Council in 1750 and, two years later, be made chief justice of the province, but these were provincial positions. Because so many of the successful merchants and lawyers had gone home and the children, who were to be pushed, must have an English education, the father decided to move his family to England. Eliza had written a friend for a certain toy "to teach him [Charles Cotesworth] according to Mr. Lock's method (which I have carefully studied) to play himself into learning. Mr. Pinckney himself has been contriving a sett of toys to teach him his letters by the time he can speak, you perceive we begin by times for he is not yet four months old." In 1753, Charles Pinckney asked to represent the colony as agent in London. When he sailed with his family, the *Gazette*, in remarking that his absence would be a loss to the province, said: "He was a true Father of his Country."

In England they resided at Ripley in Surrey, near London. But a blow befell the family at this time that was determinative of the family's career. Charles Pinckney was removed from his temporary appointment as chief justice, his place being given to Peter Leigh, who had obtained a crown appointment. It was the point at which the ambitions of placemen ran counter to those of the emerging colonial gentlemen. There was also a quarrel over the agency. In 1758 Charles Pinckney, still undecided about his future residence, returned to Carolina, where he died quite suddenly. His wife remained in Charleston to manage the family properties, not recalling her two young sons from school in England.

In his will the father requested that his elder son "be virtuously, religiously and liberally brought up, and educated in the study and practice of the Laws of England." He also directed that his younger son "shall have the same virtuous, religious and liberal education out of my estate with his brother." Eliza, never letting her sons forget their destinies, wrote Charles Cotesworth that the family depended on the progress he made "in morral Virtue, Religion and Learning." Charles Cotesworth attended Westminster, Christ Church at Oxford, the Middle Temple, and finished off his training with a tour of Europe and classes at the royal military school in Caen, France. At Oxford, he attended the lectures of Blackstone and, after sitting his terms at the Middle Temple, accompanied the judges on a country circuit. Thomas followed in his brother's footsteps, but where Charles Cotesworth excelled in Latin, Thomas became so proficient in Greek that he kept a copy of the Greek poets at hand, even on his military campaigns. Thomas was also well drilled in fencing, horsemanship, and military discipline. Although absent for over sixteen years, the young men did not lose their love of Carolina, and no doubt were often sustained by their fellow compatriots, John, Hugh, and Edward Rutledge. At the time of the Stamp Act crisis Charles Cotesworth Pinckney declaimed against the act, Zoffany capturing him and his friends on canvas in a dramatic pose of protest.

Both young men returned to Charleston before the Revolution. Within months of his return in 1769, Charles Cotesworth was elected to the Assembly from St. John's Colleton. He married Sarah Middleton, a daughter of Henry Middleton, wealthy planter and sometime royal councilor. Thomas, who came home in 1774, married Elizabeth, a granddaughter of the provincial treasurer, Jacob Motte. Somewhat earlier their sister had married Daniel Horry, one of the wealthiest planters on the Santee River. Eliza's children had acquired extensive family connections.

Both young men took an active part in military affairs. During the summer of 1775, Charles Cotesworth spent six weeks in North Carolina organizing resistance to the crown, while Thomas recruited in Orangeburg district. They were commissioned captains in the South Carolina regiments, later of the Continental line, Charles Cotesworth being the senior captain, and, after the defense of Charleston in 1776, a colonel. The brothers helped to take Fort Johnson and to fortify Haddrell's Point, their knowledge of fortifications being of special service. During the lull in the South, Charles Cotesworth served on George Washington's staff, but in 1778 he returned to join his brother in an expedition against St. Augustine. The expedition failed, and with the advance of the British under General Augustine Prevost, the patriots were pushed back to Charleston. Thomas helped to stem this tide at the Stono River, and both brothers took part in the assault on Savannah. When Clinton and Arbuthnot invested Charleston, Charles Cotesworth Pinckney commanded at Fort Moultrie, while Thomas served in the horn redoubt. Both argued against surrender, but the city fell, and with its fall, Charles Cotesworth became a prisoner of war, Thomas having escaped at the last moment by undertaking a mission for General Benjamin Lincoln.

Thomas did not join Francis Marion in the swamps but Horatio Gates on the highroad to the south. At Camden, Thomas' leg was shattered. As an invalid prisoner, he was nursed by his wife and her family at Fort Motte before being returned to Charleston. Early in 1781 the entire family was in the hands of the enemy, but it was to their credit and to their future pride that at this time they did not waver in the cause. Although Thomas' plantation at Ashepoo had been laid waste in 1779 and all the family properties confiscated in September, 1780, when Eliza was driven from her home on the Bay, Charles Cotesworth still wrote from Snee Farm, his cousin's estate where he was interned, to a British officer who asked him to change sides: "I entered into this Cause after much reflection, & through principle, my heart is altogether American." In late spring, 1781, the two brothers were exchanged and went to Philadelphia with their families. At the end of the war Charles Cotesworth was a brigadier general, and Thomas was recruiting in Virginia.

Although they had not distinguished themselves by any great military exploits, they had consistently served the cause and had established an honorable military tradition. As officers of the Continental line, they were eligible to join the Society of Cincinnati, which they did when it was formed in South Carolina. Some thought that the Cincinnati might use military rank as the basis for establishing a new American aristocracy. There was no more outspoken pamphlet than the one Aedanus Burke wrote in 1783 to counter this glaring inconsistency in the Revolutionary story. While Ramsay hoped for an end to slavery, Burke hoped for an end to privileged classes. The Pinckneys silently pushed both protests aside. The annual meetings of the Cincinnati, with their public parades and special orations, became features of the new society, the members of the Cincinnati the most glittering ornaments. The two brothers served as third and fourth presidents-general of the Cincinnati, succeeding Washington and Alexander Hamilton. Charles Cotesworth returned to head the southern half of the army in the crisis of 1799, and Thomas returned to service in 1812 to command the southeastern army. Both were to have their portraits painted in full military regalia.

During the 1780's both brothers devoted themselves to the restoration of the family fortunes. They resumed the practice of law, in which Charles Cotesworth was soon preeminent in the city. Miranda, the Spanish patriot, who observed both, felt that the elder brother was "a man of good judgment, profound knowledge in his profession, and strength in his arguments, although his eloquence is neither as brilliant nor as sonorous as that of [Edward Rutledge]." The younger brother was "not yet complete in anything, although many believe him to be a prodigy in everything: he has obtained a good education in Europe, is still young, and shows great promise." Thomas, who had inherited Auckland plantation on the Ashepoo and had bought Fairfield and Eldorado on the Santee, gave up the law for planting. Charles Cotesworth, even though he had bought two of the confiscated estates with his brother-in-law, Edward Rutledge, continued to practice at the bar. There was a great deal of money to be made out of untying the property entanglements left over from the war, as well as from serving the mercantile community. When the Duke de la Rochefoucauld-Liancourt visited Charleston in 1796, he listed Charles Cotesworth Pinckney and Edward Rutledge as being at the head of the bar and earning from £3,500 to £4,500 sterling a year.

The most important role that the members of the Pinckney family ever played was that of delegates to the Constitutional Convention in 1787. At this convention South Carolina was represented by four men, all Charlestonians, two of whom were Pinckneys, Charles Cotesworth and his first cousin once removed, Charles Pinckney. This young man, who was twenty-nine in 1787, was the heir of a no less distinguished tradition than his cousins.

Charles was the grandson of William Pinckney (1704-66), Indian trader and provincial officeholder. William Pinckney went bankrupt in 1744 and lived out the remainder of his days as commissary-general, suffering, toward the last, from a stroke of palsy. In 1725 he had married Ruth Brewton, the daughter of the powder receiver. His eldest son, Thomas, had seen service during the French and Indian War in Canada, Martinique, and Cuba, having been wounded on the plains of Abraham. The second son, Charles (1732-82), was intended by the uncle as his heir, until his marriage to Eliza Lucas in 1744. Eliza wrote in her letters that her husband continued to sponsor his nephew in his studies of the law, the young man never showing disappointment in his missed fortune. This Charles Pinckney married his cousin Frances Brewton, became a lawyer, and played a far more prominent role in the first days of the Revolution than did his first cousins. In December,

1773, he was one of the committee demanding that the consignees of the tea turn their cargoes over to the agents of the Assembly. Yet by July, 1774, he was identified with the more conservative wing of the patriot party. He and his brother-in-law, Miles Brewton, were defeated by Henry Middleton and Edward Rutledge, the father-in-law and the brother-in-law of Charles Cotesworth Pinckney, for seats on the delegation to the First Continental Congress. In 1775 and 1776, although Charles Pinckney headed some of the extralegal committees, he was reluctant to cut the tie with England. After the fall of Charleston in 1780, he took protection. It has been said that this course cut him off from his cousins; it certainly brought about the amercement of his estate at Jacksonborough. Yet in September, 1782, when he died, Charles Cotesworth Pinckney wrote in high praise of his cousin's character.

Although the young Charles Pinckney (1757–1824) had spent some time in a prison ship in Charleston harbor for his part in the defense of the city, he suffered the loss of some of his property, though by no means any sizable portion. Young Charles Pinckney, still a very rich man, was a brilliant example of self-education, for, because of the Revolution, he was unable to attend the Inns of Court and was educated at home under the direction of Dr. David Olyphant. In the 1780's he made a name for himself first in the state legislature and then as delegate to the Congress from South Carolina. By 1786 he was working harder than anyone else to keep that body intact. When New Jersey failed to contribute her requisition, Congress sent him to urge her to comply. In the summer of 1786 he offered to Congress itself a set of seven amendments to the Articles of Confederation, designed to strengthen what was already a moribund body. These amendments were one important prelude to the Constitution of 1787.

The South Carolina delegation to the Philadelphia convention was a family affair. Besides the two cousins, there was John Rutledge, whose brother, Edward, was Charles Cotesworth Pinckney's brother-in-law, and Pierce Butler, whose wife was a Middleton, cousin to the wives of Charles Cotesworth Pinckney and Edward Rutledge. Henry Laurens, who had been selected as the fifth member of the delegation, did not attend. In 1788 his daughter Eleanor married Charles Pinckney.

The gentlemen who met in Philadelphia in 1787 shared a common experience which had begun in New York in 1765 and had been strengthened in Philadelphia in 1774 and 1775. John Adams may have been harsh in his strictures against the Rutledges, but the New Englanders needed the South Carolinians in 1774, and they made a significant concession when they permitted rice to be excepted from the nonexportation agreement. From this concession may have stemmed the feeling that southern agricultural products were needed. The bonds of common experience were forged more deeply during the Revolution, and this wartime association had been continued in the days after the Revolution. Many of Greene's officers married rice heiresses: William Washington, Lewis Morris, Dr. Henry Collins Flagg. Even more important was the fact that the men mingled during their summer vacations in New York and Newport. The geography of the eighteenth century brought South Carolina closer to New England and New York than it ever did to Virginia.

What strengthened this geography of the days of sail

was the geography of trade. Among these gentlemen it was understood that the new nation needed the southern staples to fill the New England vessels and to trade in Europe for the things wanted in the new country. It was also an axiom with most of the American gentlemen that these crops could only be grown by slave labor. Therefore, Charles Cotesworth Pinckney did not primarily see the need for protection in the Constitution for southern interests, once concessions on slavery had been made by eastern gentlemen. Undoubtedly, the southern Federalists were men who believed that gentlemen would keep their word. But even if New Englanders did not keep their word on slavery, South Carolinians had quite extraordinary faith in their own abilities to control the situation. Had they not the classical heroes and seventeenth-century English heroes as models? And had they not themselves won the Revolution? William L. Smith continually extolled the great efforts of South Carolina in contrast to those of Virginia.

It was Charles Pinckney who first saw the southern economic interest as hostile to, not supplemental to, the northern economic interests. In the Philadelphia convention, he delineated five major economic interests in the United States: the fisheries and West Indian trade of New England, the interests of the free port of New York, the wheat and flour trade of Pennsylvania and New Jersey, the tobacco of Maryland and Virginia, and the rice and indigo of the Carolinas and Georgia. He wanted constitutional guarantees, not the word of gentlemen, to protect the state's interest. Consequently, he worked for a three-fourths vote as necessary for the passage of any navigation act. Although this measure failed, the provision for a two-thirds vote to ratify treaties gave some protection. Perhaps because he was a young man and an intellectual, he could see to the heart of the matter more easily than his older cousins, who had sailed more smoothly through the Revolution. Charles Pinckney pointed the way to Calhoun. Benjamin Franklin suggested that each delegation go home and fight for the document in a unanimous fashion as though there had been no divisions on the floor of the convention, and that was what the South Carolina delegation did. The differences among the Pinckneys were temporarily covered up.

Governor Thomas Pinckney received the work of the convention and called a special session of the legislature to consider the calling of a ratification convention. After debate, the calling of the convention was approved. The convention met in May, with Thomas Pinckney presiding as chairman. Both in the legislature in January, 1788, and in the convention in May, 1788, the Pinckneys, along with their allies, the Rutledges, fought for ratification. The Rutledge-Pinckney faction was a key group in a crucial state. They won the battle with arguments emphasizing the need for protection from foreigners and debtors, rather than the need for protection from the North. To celebrate, there was a grand procession through the streets of the city, ending on Federal Green.

Charleston was now at the peak of her importance. Without the city, the state would not have been for ratification. Without South Carolina, there would have been no United States. The city's wealth paralleled her new importance, for this decade produced the last of her great merchants and her largest number of artisans. The Pinckneys, who had plantations in the outlying parishes, also had homes in the city: Charles Cotesworth in the ancestral home on Colleton Square, Charles on lower Meeting Street, and Thomas in his new showplace on George Street. They filled these homes with the most exquisite furnishings of the day, particularly with those things all three brought back from their diplomatic missions to Europe. Satisfaction should have been the Pinckney hallmark.

Yet it was Charles Pinckney who, as governor, had to deal with the events in Santo Domingo which were to have a shaping influence on the mind of the city. The great slave revolt took place in 1791, and soon Charleston was overrun by refugees from that island. They were welcomed into the local society for their musical and artistic talents, but they also brought their fears. As late as 1820, there was one elegant old French lady in the madhouse who had lost her mind in the holocaust when her husband and children were butchered. As the owner of seven plantations and countless slaves and as governor of a slave state, Charles Pinckney became worried about the threat of an attack being launched from that island upon the southern parts of the United States. This threat had ominous portents for southern commerce, property, and slaves.

Eliza Pinckney, at the time of the French and Indian War, had written that her husband intended to return to Carolina for two years in order to dispose of his property there and "fix it in a more secure tho' less improvable part of the world." When she heard that a fleet was headed for America, she had written: "We flatter ourselves they will take the Mississippi in their way, which if they succeed in must put an end to all our Indian Warrs, as they could never molest us if ye french from thence did not supply them with arms and ammunition." Her sons, in the 1790's, proceeded to remove the cause of these fears by making diplomatic arrangements which would finally secure the place of Charleston in this southern world. If the threats from the West Indies could be curtailed and the mouth of the Mississippi secured, then the nation could grow to the west and the slave interest be protected.

Whereas the Pinckneys had not been consulted by the royal authorities, they were by President Washington. He offered them, in turn, judgeships, cabinet posts, and diplomatic missions. In 1791, Thomas was appointed minister to London. There he took his family, leaving his brother to manage the family properties at home. Thomas was to secure American commercial rights and compensation for 25,000 slaves taken away in 1782. John Jay, who had no interest in slavery and who had once been willing to bargain away United States rights on the Mississippi, was ultimately sent to negotiate the treaty with Britain. This appointment almost alienated the Pinckneys, for it came at the time when their friend John Rutledge was being rejected for the chief justiceship of the United States, an incident reminiscent of their father's experience in the 1750's. Charles Pinckney was vehement against the Jay Treaty; Charles Cotesworth Pinckney had to exercise all of his self-control in order to remain neutral. The Washington administration saved itself with the Pinckneys by appointing Thomas to a special mission to Spain and Charles Cotesworth Pinckney as minister to France. Thomas quickly reached an agreement whereby Spain moved back her southern frontier and permitted navigation of the Mississippi. The Pinckney Treaty opened up the choicest slave territory of the future to the southern states, which the rapaciousness of the Yazoo men soon exploited. Thomas' success brought him second place on the Federalist ticket in 1796.

Charles Cotesworth Pinckney had been Francophile and

hoped for an accommodation with France, but he was not amused by the revolutionary fervor, especially as it was manifested in Santo Domingo. Yet it was only after he was driven out of France and then, upon his return, insulted by the demands of a bribe that he fell into the arms of the high Federalists at home. His slogan—"No, no, not a sixpence"—became a rallying cry. He generously gave way to Hamilton as the ranking officer and joined with the Federalists to prepare the army for war. At home, Castle Pinckney, on Shute's Folly, was fortified, ships were offered to the government, and great welcomes were prepared for the returning Pinckneys. Thomas' carriage was unhorsed and dragged through the streets by the jubilant citizens; Charles Cotesworth extended a handsome banquet.

And yet, Charles Pinckney, sitting in Charleston as governor and then in Philadelphia as senator, thought his cousins were being duped by the leaders of the national party. Did not Hamilton try desperately to use Thomas in 1796 and Charles Cotesworth in 1800? Peter Porcupine made insinuations about Thomas' mission to England, while "The Tale of the Tub" cast a bad light over Charles Cotesworth's activities in France. Was not the Adams administration ready to agree to a Negro republic to the south? Had the brothers forgotten that they were defending southern interests?

Charles Pinckney began to see what was coming while he was in the Senate. His speeches, published in 1800, reflected his fears. He was against sending judges on foreign missions and against allowing federal marshals to summon jurors; the corruption of the judicial branch would be the result of such practices. He was against giving the President discretionary power to cut off commercial intercourse with France and her dependencies, for that gave the President too much power over southern interests. He defended the exclusive rights of the state legislatures to select senators and presidential electors; nor could Congress decide disputed presidential elections. These would be threats to the independence of the states. He was against the sedition law, for, "The press is to a free people, *the tree of the knowledge of good and evil.*"

Charles Pinckney spoke more essentially for the agrarian interests. William Smith's mercantile constituency was to wane and even to disappear, a factor which undermined the strength of the Pinckneys and the Rutledges. The grand battle was in 1800, when Charles Pinckney achieved a victory for Jefferson in South Carolina against funds, banks, the British, and the old guard. And Charles Pinckney had not disdained to raise the tradesmen and the backcountrymen against his cousins in that election—a new brand of politics that could only sap the strength of leaders buttressed by deference. His reward was the mission to Spain, but Madrid was too far from home, especially since Florida could not be secured at this time.

In his 1808 message to the state legislature, which brought to a close his fourth term as governor of the state, the nagging worries that beset Charles Pinckney were further revealed. Pointing out that most of the legislators were planters, he said that they should be concerned with the hostile designs of the French in the West Indies. The militia was organized into brigades and those on the coast alerted. The fort on Sullivan's Island had been reconstructed by Colonel Christian Senf, and three gunboats contributed by subscription for the protection of the coast. More interestingly, and as a prelude to the Missouri debates, he wanted a law to prevent free persons of color from coming in from the West Indies and another law stating that no pass for a slave to leave the state would be given without the owner signing the pass in front of a notary.

The younger members of the Federalist party saw a need to adopt the tactics of their opponents if they were to win again, as David Fischer has pointed out in *The Revolution of American Conservatism*. Bitter battles were the result, becoming almost internecine as Charles Pinckney battled John Rutledge, Jr. Mrs. Gabriel Manigault's letters are shot through with the bitterness of party battles in this first decade of the nineteenth century. Society was split, and Republicans ostracized by the old guard. When William Loughton Smith succumbed to the shifting pressures and changed sides, he was cut off immediately. Mrs. Manigault wrote to her son, "Remember that and fear it!" The old Jockey Club generals saw the new politics as only bad, raising up new forces from the depths of society. Perhaps this was why, in 1804 and again in 1808, Charles Cotesworth Pinckney did not raise a hand to secure his own election as President. No presidential candidate sat more still. Imagine directing a political campaign from the fastness of Pinckney Island, a day's journey from Charleston!

But just as these party battles might have raised up a strong two-party system in South Carolina, the society underneath coalesced through natural changes into a new unity. The spread of cotton, after the invention of the gin in 1793, was phenomenal. And with the spread of cotton into the uplands, slavery followed, the demand for slaves forcing an opening of the slave trade between 1803 and 1808, an opening desired not by the rice planters below but by the cotton farmers above who were eager to rise to the level of their Charleston opponents. Soon these up-country farmers were marrying their daughters to Charleston nabobs. Successful farmers gobbled up the land of their neighbors, who moved either west or, in the case of the Quakers who disliked slavery, to the northwest. Men, such as Charles Cotesworth Pinckney, saw this as a good thing and proceeded to found a college in Columbia where the new backcountry elite could be indoctrinated with the same ideas as those held by lowcountrymen. The new unity was sanctioned in 1808 with a more equitable division in representation in the legislature and in 1810 by the adoption of white manhood suffrage which, by then, was no step toward democracy, for the deferential society was working as well in the backcountry as it had ever worked on the coast.

But one question still worried the leaders. Could the bitter personal political fights continue? There could be rivalry among the elite if the society itself was isolated from national battles. But if a national party should use an issue detrimental to local society, that issue might pry the local society apart. When the northern Federalists took up the slavery issue at the time of the Missouri controversy in order to make a comeback nationally, the Carolina leaders had to think twice about allegiance to any national party. It was again Charles Pinckney who, by his speeches in Congress in 1819–20, sounded the alarm.

The point which concerned Pinckney most was not whether Missouri should come in as a slave state but whether, after she became a state, she could bar free Negroes and mulattoes from her borders. To northern spokesmen, such an exclusion was a violation of the privileges and immunities clause in the Constitution of the United States.

136

To be one people, one nation, each person in it should be free to move about—mobility being a cherished American freedom. One of the privileges and immunities guaranteed the citizen of each state was the ability to move from place to place, to find a job, to support himself. It was at this point that Charles Pinckney began the tradition of constitutionalism within the city and the state. Being one of the few members of the Philadelphia convention still living, he could speak with authority, especially since he claimed to have introduced this clause into the Constitution. It was his interpretation that no one had intended for that clause to include free Negroes. If his interpretation was correct, a state—his own or Missouri—might bar the entry of such persons. In 1808 he had advised his own legislature to bar free persons of color coming from the West Indies. Pinckney was raising the question of the nature of the union—was this one nation of equal individuals, or was it a group of states? John Marshall, in thunderous decisions in 1819 and 1821, was stating that it was one nation. South Carolina began to see in the Court an institution that might try to decide this all-important question. Had it not been Burke, a South Carolinian in Congress, who had objected to calling the head of the Court chief justice—too awesome a title! Even though Bruce and De Brahm had been unable to build a canal across the Neck, Charleston was becoming a city-state, and city-states implied lack of mobility.

And then there came in the 1820's the economic decline of South Carolina and of Charleston. The North no longer needed southern economic support. What was revealed was a bitter rivalry between the ports, with New York winning at the expense of Charleston, among others. All those groups in Charleston which had supported the federalism of Smith had been drained off in the direction of New York. And now there seemed little capital to invest in new schemes to remedy the situation.

These economic changes had begun in Charleston in 1808. The foreign slave trade came to an end; foreign commerce, in general, was cut off by the embargo. In New England there was a shift to industry. Charleston, which had been at the center of the Atlantic world of commerce, would not be at the center of the new age of industry. William Loughton Smith, for many years her congressman, tried to warn the city at the time of the dedication of the site for Charleston's first manufacturing establishment, a homespun company, but the city did not consider the warnings, and the factory failed. The changes of 1808 to 1815 were somewhat blurred and forgotten amid the boom prices for sea island cotton between 1815 and 1819. Fortunes were made in those days, and new mansions were erected in Charleston and on the islands to the south. Charles Cotesworth Pinckney experimented with the crop on Pinckney Island. But the panic of 1819, the Missouri Compromise debates of 1820, and the Denmark Vesey insurrection of 1822 jolted the city and changed ultimately her way of life—from a city that had looked outward to one that henceforth looked inward.

The change from sail to steam left Charleston behind, far from the main east-west Atlantic Ocean routes. In 1819 her sister city sent the *Savannah*, under Captain Moses Rogers, across the ocean as an experiment in more direct means of communication. As long as South Carolina was herself a leading cotton producer as she was from 1793 to 1820, Charleston might be the port for the staple, but when the rich lands of Alabama and Mississippi began to yield their crops, as they did in the 1820's, she was no longer the master of this new and more important staple. She had been *the* rice port, but she was never *the* cotton port. She could be saved as a city only by canals or railroads or expertise. Canals had been tried, first with the Santee and then with the Catawba companies, but they had brought no returns to the private investors, nor had they bridged the mountains.

In 1817 the state set up a commission, under the direction of Robert Mills, to tackle the problem of transportation. The dreams were large—a line of waterways and roads from the Cooper River across the continent to the Columbia River, with Charleston as the entrance to this northwest passage—but the results were small. She would try railroads later. But, as for expertise, this was the period when New York City was proving that she had it. Her financial institutions were being transformed to sustain a speculative economy. Her agents and those of Boston and Providence came south to buy up the crops to fill the ships those cities were sending to England. The New England Society was founded in 1819 in Charleston. When New York began regular weekly packet crossings, she could give service which Charleston's great merchants, many of whom had retired during the dark days after 1808, could not give. When the Erie Canal was completed in 1825 just as South Carolina's efforts were failing, there was no stopping her. Failing to keep up with modern changes and becoming sensitive to criticism about slavery, Charleston underwent a transformation from the spaciousness of the eighteenth century to the inbreeding of the nineteenth.

The other ominous force appearing in the 1820's was the rise of Jackson and a new brand of popular politics, in which demagogues directly appealed to the people for their votes. In such politics, gentlemen could find no place. What would happen when the new brand of popular politics found an issue (supported not merely by the northern aristocratic Federalists but by the mass of the people) such as slavery—particularly after it was discovered that the North did not need the South in any economic sense?

Within the state there must be unity, and politics must be played as the Federalists had envisaged it. All institutions should bolster the natural leaders of society—the churches, schools, local government. Outside the state the game should be played as Charles Pinckney had suggested and as Calhoun would expound it. Constitutional guarantees must serve in the new world for the word of a gentleman in the world that had passed. The position of the Charleston leaders was set and that of the state and of the South too.

VI.

The Closed City

THE ABORTIVE DENMARK VESEY insurrection in 1822 stirred Charleston in much the same way as the Missouri debates in 1820 had stirred the nation. It raised questions about the future of the city's society and, more immediately, about the place of the free Negro and the slave in that city.

Negro slaves had come to the city with the first settlers. When they grew in numbers as the rice fields expanded along the coast, the fear of Negro insurrection grew in the mind of the white man. With the first really large importations, the province thought it necessary to balance the Negro influx with a tide of poor Protestants from Europe. After the Stono slave uprising of 1739, just south of the city, a comprehensive slave code was enacted into law, a code which lasted with very few changes until the Civil War. Periodically the slave trade was cut off by prohibitive duties, to reduce the numbers of slaves being purchased and thereby to reduce the debts of the planters. In 1761 there were 4,000 white persons and 4,000 Negro slaves in the city. In 1790 there were 8,089 whites, 7,684 slaves, and 568 free Negroes—a total of 16,341. In 1820 there were 11,229 whites, 12,652 slaves, and 1,475 free Negroes—a total of 25,356. In 1850 there were 20,012 whites, 19,532 slaves, and 3,441 free Negroes—a total of 42,985.

At the beginning of the Revolution the foreign slave trade was cut off by the Continental Congress. South Carolina, having imported large numbers during the early 1770's, was not averse to this action. There was, for the moment, the possibility that liberty might be contagious, and the slaves be freed. Henry Laurens, in a notable letter to his son John, advocated emancipation, but the southerners blocked any statement concerning slavery in the Declaration of Independence. When General Greene was hard pressed in 1781, he asked if he might arm the South Carolina slaves. John Laurens approved, suggesting that freedom might be the slaves' reward; but the Rutledges opposed and carried the day.

After the Revolution the slave trade was reopened, but the trade was closed again in 1787 by state action. However, in the Constitutional Convention in 1787, Charles Cotesworth Pinckney fought for the preservation of the right to import slaves until 1808. What might have been progressive steps toward emancipation came to an end in the 1790's, the decade in which the citizens were forgetting their revolutionary fervor and lapsing into southern ways. The great slave insurrection in Santo Domingo sent a distinct chill of horror through the southern white community. The rise of a black republic, with a black Napoleon, Toussaint L'Ouverture, was an ominous example. Santo Domingan refugees, pouring into Charleston, took jobs as dressmakers, music masters, and teachers, started a newspaper, *Le Patriote Français*, and strengthened, by their presence, the Catholic congregation on Hasell Street—thereby adding to the culture and to the fears of the city. The fire of 1796 was thought to have been set by a Negro arsonist, the servant of a West Indian refugee. On May 5, 1798, a mass meeting was held in St. Michael's Church to discuss what the people thought was a threatened attack from Santo Domingo. The rice planters with homes in Charleston never seriously thought of emancipation, but when the upcountry farmers found a need for slaves in order to plant cotton, the state became more firmly fixed in its views.

Among the groups in the city the Methodists alone favored emancipation. John Wesley and Francis Asbury were both opponents of slavery. Asbury, on his many visits to Charleston in the decades after the Revolution, laid the basis for the Methodist church in that city, teaching along the way his abolitionist views.

A group of twenty-three Methodist ministers, who circulated among the lowcountry parishes as itinerant preachers, met in Charleston in January, 1795, and drew up a powerful statement: "Whereas We the Ministers of the Methodist Episcl. Church, being deeply sensible of the impropriety, & evil of Slavery, in itself. And its baneful consequences, on Religious Society. And as some formerly professing the same sentiments, have Nevertheless afterwards upon a change of circumstances become the patrons of Slavery; as well as the holders of Slaves themselves; To the Scandal of the Ministry, and the strengthening of the hands of Oppression. Do agree that all such persons amongst us. Who are Now, or may hereafter become the Possessors of Slaves. Ought Immediately to Emancipate them where the Laws will permit it: And where They will Not, that they Ought to make them compensation for their Labour; And *will* them free;—And we are resolved that Every Member of this Association. Who shall act otherwise, Shall forfeit both his seat in conference, and Letters of Ordination."

These views were not popular ones, as David Ramsay discovered when he was defeated for public office, largely because of his known sympathies for the abolition of slavery. When the Methodists compromised in 1804 by accepting two disciplines, one for the northern churches and another for the southern churches, the only strong force in opposition to slavery was removed. A few African Methodist churches were formed in Charleston around 1804, but they were the strongholds of the free Negro community, a small minority in the city. By a city ordinance of October 28, 1806, assemblies of more than seven free persons of color must be attended by a white person, nor could free persons of color assemble for dancing or "other merriment" without written permission of the warden of the ward.

Emancipation, which in the eighteenth century was quite easy in South Carolina by will or deed, became less easy after the law of 1800, which required scrutiny of character and special deed before emancipation, and almost impossible after 1820, when a special law of the legislature was henceforth required for each emancipation. At the time of the Missouri debates it became apparent that the free Negro was not to be permitted to move freely from one state of the Union to another. When the mobility of the free Negro in the nation was thus threatened, the free Negroes living in Charleston alleys began to feel society closing in upon them.

The important thing about the Denmark Vesey insurrection was not whether there had been a plot but what the white population of the city thought had been happening in the free Negro community which might have effects upon the slave community. They thought ideas were seeping in. Had not Denmark Vesey spent his life sailing on Captain Joseph Vesey's schooner between Charleston and West Indian ports, even to the ports of Santo Domingo? Had not the leaders of the African Methodist Church made many trips back and forth between Charleston and the North? Had not the Missouri debates been discussed among

144

the free Negroes themselves? The executions of Denmark Vesey, the only free Negro to be executed, and of the thirty-six slaves were intended to be a warning to both free and slave Negroes.

A great shift now took place in the mind of the Charlestonians. The citizens had once suspected a conspiracy in the men around George III; now they saw one among the abolitionists. Tyranny, as always for South Carolinians, threatened from afar. Where they had once sought stability in the word of gentlemen and in a balance within the state between low and upcountry, they now must achieve stability by suppression. Old Thomas Pinckney, who had once stopped a mutiny by sabering the ringleader, wrote a pamphlet under the pseudonym of "Achates," urging firmness with the slaves and closure of the channels through which ideas were percolating through the city. The South Carolina legislature, as if reflecting the latter view, passed Seamen's Acts in 1822 and 1823, which henceforth required free Negroes on all vessels coming to the port of Charleston to be placed in jail upon arrival and kept there until their departure. If the master of the vessel did not pay for their board and room, the Negroes might be sold into slavery in order to pay for the cost of the enforced lodgings. No longer could free Negroes enter the state, nor could free Negroes who departed return to the state. Thus, in attempting to seal off the state, South Carolina came into conflict with the nation and the outside world. From this time forth, Charleston began to create a closed society.

In 1823 a free Negro sailing on a British vessel tested the seamen's laws in the federal courts in Charleston. Henry Elkinson, when imprisoned, petitioned for a writ of habeas corpus. Judge William Johnson thought the state's Seamen's Acts were unconstitutional and so stated, but, on the basis of technicalities, the state's program was upheld. The protest of the British minister through Washington was not effective. Later, when Judge Hoare of Massachusetts arrived to uphold the rights of free Negroes on New England vessels, he was run out of the city. Obviously British and New England ships made fewer calls at Charleston. This situation brought a further decline in the commerce of the city.

There was, of course, a need for internal police. When the Duke of Saxe-Weimar visited the city during the winter of 1825–26, he inspected the institutions that had been set up to control the slaves and described them in his memoirs. He had come to visit the Germans, mostly tradesmen of small capital but of great respectability, who had come during the preceding fifty years. Some sixty persons gave the Duke a three o'clock dinner at the rooms of the German Friendly Society, which had been founded by the Wurtemberger Captain Michael Kalteisen, to provide a school for the children of its members. Colonel Jacob Sass, a Hessian, and John Siegling from Erfurt (who had established a music store where he sold harps, pianos, and wind instruments) were his hosts. Charles Strohecker escorted the Duke to the Lutheran Church to hear the Rev. John Bachman preach. This immigrant group, efficient, tidy, and educated, had accepted the local society.

The Duke stopped at Jones's Hotel, situated on Broad Street behind St. Michael's Church and run by the mulatto Jehu Jones, whose wife had gone north and had not been permitted to return. Since the hotel was quite near the Watch House, located on the southwest corner of Broad and Meeting streets, the Duke could observe closely the watch: "Charleston keeps in pay a company of police soldiers, who during the night occupy several posts. . . . This corps owes its support to the fear of the negroes. At nine o'clock in the evening a bell is sounded; and after this no negro can venture without a written permission from his master, or he will immediately be thrown into prison, nor can his owner obtain his release till next day, by the payment of a fine. Should the master refuse to pay this fine, then the slave receives twenty-five lashes, and a receipt, with which he is sent back to his master."

A second guardhouse was established in the 1820's on the site of the tobacco-inspection warehouses, which were no longer needed, because of the decline in tobacco production in South Carolina. It was out of this guardhouse that a military institution to train the young men grew. After The Citadel opened in 1843 in the very center of the city, on Sundays, the cadets marched in groups to the churches of their choice, an always reassuring sight to the citizens and an awe-inspiring one to the Negroes.

Of even more importance for keeping the slaves under control was the Work House with its flogging block and treadmill. The Work House, still situated on the Mazyck lands, was an old institution in the city, but the Duke gave a detailed description of the innovations in use there: "I found the other prison, destined for the punishment of minor offences of the negro slaves, in a better condition. In it there were about forty individuals of both sexes. These slaves are either such as have been arrested during the night by the police, or such as have been sent here by their masters for punishment. The house displays throughout a remarkable neatness; black overseers go about every where armed with cowhides. In the basement story there is an apparatus upon which the negroes, by order of the police, or at the request of their masters, are flogged. The latter can have nineteen lashes inflicted on them according to the existing law. The machine consists of a sort of crane, on which a cord with two nooses runs over pullies; the nooses are made fast to the hands of the slave and drawn up, while the feet are bound tight to a plank. The body is stretched out as much as possible, and thus the miserable creature receives the exact number of lashes as counted off! Within a year, flogging occurs less frequently: that is to say, a tread-mill has been erected in a back building of the prison, in which there are two treadwheels in operation. Each employs twelve prisoners, who work a mill for grinding corn, and thereby contribute to the support of the prison. Six tread at once upon each wheel, while six rest upon a bench placed behind the wheel. Every half minute the left hand man steps off the treadwheel, while the five others move to the left to fill up the vacant place; at the same time the right hand man sitting on the bench, steps on the wheel, and begins his movement, while the rest, sitting on the bench, uniformly recede. Thus, even three minutes sitting, allows the uphappy being no repose. The signal for changing is given by a small bell attached to the wheel. The prisoners are compelled to labour eight hours a day in this manner. Order is preserved by a person, who, armed with a cow-hide, stands by the wheel. Both sexes tread promiscuously upon the wheel, Since, however, only twenty-four prisoners find employment at once on both wheels, the idle are obliged in the interval to sit upon a floor in the upper chambers, and observe a strict silence. One who had eloped several times from a plantation, was fastened by a heavy iron ring, that passed over his leg to the floor. To provide against this state of idleness, there should be another pair of tread-wheels erected. The negroes entertain a strong fear of the tread-mills, and regard flogging as the lighter evil! Of about three hundred and sixty, who, since the erection of these tread-mills, have been employed upon them, only six have been sent back a second time."

It was the knowledge of what went on in the Work House that drove Sarah and Angelina Grimké into the arms of the abolitionists. When Theodore Weld published *American Slavery As It Is* in 1839, the most powerful indictment of the institution until the publication of *Uncle Tom's Cabin*, the Grimké sisters supplied stories about punishments in the Work House.

Since it was the presence of large numbers of Negro slaves in the city that caused the attitudes of the citizens to change, one might have expected much support in Charleston for the American Colonization Society's movement to send the Negroes back to Africa. This movement originally, in 1817, had support in Charleston. The Rev. Christopher Gadsden, rector of St. Philip's and later bishop of South Carolina, served as local agent and collected over five hundred dollars from leading Charlestonians, but, as one writer commented, "The green stalk of colonization shriveled in the heat of the Missouri debates." General Charles Cotesworth Pinckney later recanted his endorsement. At the end of the decade, when there was a move to secure federal funds to underwrite the Society's aims, there was a veritable outburst of resentment against the Society. Robert Turnbull in his "Crisis" papers, James Hamilton, Jr. in the state legislature, Robert Y. Hayne in the United States Senate all condemned the movement. Judge William Harper, writing for the new *Southern Review* in 1828, agreed with the author of the "Crisis" that the aim of the Society was emancipation: "It was the 'Amis des Noirs' who set on foot the insurrection of St. Domingo." The Charleston *Mercury* condemned the movement as one hatched by abolitionists to breed "anxiety, inquietude and troubles to which there could be no end." Only Thomas Smith Grimké continued to support the idea of colonization until his death in 1834.

Instead of removing the slaves, the planters turned toward a mission to the slaves. The Rev. Charles Cotesworth Pinckney, the son of General Thomas Pinckney, opened the movement with a speech in 1829 to the South Carolina Agricultural Society, in which he tried to convince the planters that they should Christianize their slaves. "Nothing is better calculated to render man satisfied with his destiny in this world than a conviction that its hardships and trials are as transitory as its honors and enjoyments." Just as slave morality would be improved, so the institution of slavery would be improved. Then the South could refute northern criticisms. The Rev. Charles Cotesworth Pinckney, who implemented these views on his own ancestral lands along the Santee River, succeeded in winning many planters to this mission, which the Methodists took up as a balm to soothe their own troubled consciences.

With the future bleak, the city in economic decline, and old fears revitalized, the citizens turned to their historic past for reassurance. The heroes of the Revolution had fought against tyranny; their descendants would do the same. What was therefore necessary was a history that ensured heroes, and so there began, in the 1820's in Charleston, the idolization of the Revolutionary figures. Myths were manufactured out of good material. This was the day of Parson Weems's *George Washington* and *Francis*

Marion, but the key work in South Carolina hagiography was Major Alexander Garden's *Anecdotes of the Revolutionary War*, which appeared in 1822 and was reprinted in 1828. Major Garden dedicated his work to the Pinckneys. "My object, in giving publicity to the Anecdotes I would record, is, avowedly, to honour the Fathers of our Revolution, and to excite that emulation in their descendants, to imitate their example, that will best secure the benefits resulting from their valour, and their virtues." Garden's volume begins with the story of William Moultrie and his famous band on Sullivan's Island. The author compared them to Leonidas and those who stood at Thermopylae. William Washington was Marcellus; the prisoners on board the *Torbay* and the *Pack-Horse* akin to Regulus; the "Demosthenian eloquence" of John Rutledge was compared to the "Ciceronian style" of his brother Edward. The classics had always supplied examples, but now to the ancients would be added the modern heroes. The stories of Francis Marion and the sweet potatoes, of Andrew Jackson and the officer's boots, of Sergeant Jasper and the flag, and of Rebecca Motte and the flaming arrows stud the book. If Andrew Jackson, by his victory at New Orleans, had become a "symbol for an age," Garden was creating symbols for a city.

When Judge William Johnson wrote, in the 1820's, his biography of General Greene, he admitted that there were differences in feeling between his own times and those Revolutionary days. Johnson, who could look with favor on Greene and treat him dispassionately, not letting the guerrilla leaders Sumter and Marion usurp too much of the narrative, was still appalled by the idea that Greene wanted to arm the slaves.

Concerning General Greene's letter of December, 1781, suggesting the use of Negro troops to Governor Rutledge, Johnson wrote: "Those who can enter into the feelings and opinions of the citizens of those states which tolerate slavery, will be not a little startled at the proposition submitted to the governor and council, in this letter. A strong, deep-seated feeling, nurtured from earliest infancy, decides, with instinctive promptness, against a measure of so threatening an aspect, and so offensive to that republican pride, which disdains to commit the defence of the country to servile hands; or share with a colour, to which the idea of inferiority is inseparably connected, the profession of arms; and that approximation of condition which must exist between the regular soldier and the militia man."

"Republican pride" would not permit a country to be defended by "servile hands." In 1860, after thirty years of such drilling in the classics, ancient and modern, the young men of the city were ready to fight and never to think of calling upon their slaves to fight beside them.

Such history must challenge all attempts to reveal the faults of the heroes. There is no better example of this side of historical writing than Robert Y. Hayne's attempt in the 1828 issue of the *Southern Review* to refute Lord Rawdon's slurs upon the motives of Colonel Isaac Hayne. Senator Hayne did not wish apologies for Weymms, Watson, Brown, Tarleton, and Rawdon. "And thus, one by one, may our history be rifled of every incident calculated to confer honor on the American character." After the Senator had completed weighing Colonel Isaac Hayne's "moral necessity" for taking protection with Lord Rawdon's comments thereupon, he concluded: "We have now performed, as well as we were able, what we conceived a duty to the memory of one of the most revered of our martyrs. It is due to the country, that not a single trophy of the Revolution should be suffered to be destroyed, and we should be sorry to see recorded on one of them, the memorable inscription on the beautiful naval monument in Washington, 'mutilated by Britons.' We would, if we could, preserve them all, in their simple majesty and beauty, to kindle in the bosom of our American youth, to the latest posterity, the sacred glow of patriotism. We have always considered the moral and political lessons, taught by the history of the Revolution, as the most precious inheritance derived from our fathers."

In 1830, when Maria Henrietta Pinckney, the daughter of General Charles Cotesworth Pinckney, had reduced the nullification doctrine to its simplest form in *The Quintessence of Long Speeches, arranged as a Political Catechism*, she asked herself and her readers on whom could they depend. Her answer was: "On the descendants of the patriot band who achieved the Revolution."

When Judge Harper, also writing in the *Southern Review* for 1828, compared South Carolina to Santo Domingo and the abolitionists in the north to the "Amis des Noirs" in France, he also raised the question of how the South should respond. His answer was state self-reliance. "We are not St. Domingo, nor do we intend to be. . . . We are sovereign." The city would respond as it had done during the Revolution. The doctrine of nullification was fierce and unyielding, not so much because of fear, but because of pride, which, on looking back to the American Revolution, was more than half-justified. It was this pride which drove them to the Civil War and sustained them though it.

No doubt the return of Lafayette in 1825 and the funerals of both Charles Cotesworth Pinckney in 1825 and Thomas

Pinckney in 1828 gave an additional impetus to this back-ward-looking, militarily oriented thinking. What a dramatic moment when the Pinckneys descended from their carriage at the corner of Meeting and George streets to embrace their old comrade! What memories of the past rose in the minds of all Charlestonians who watched the parade wind through the streets of Charleston shaded by the pride of India trees. The young William Gilmore Simms, in his first publication, wrote of General Charles Cotesworth Pinckney as "that giant oak" who had gone. The young poet realized that the "godlike few" would not be forgotten: "But memory, colder still, each object bears,/ Renew'd, and glowing thro' the vale of years. . . ."

What was developing was a certain reverence for the past, a living to protect that past, a rigidity, an inflexibility. The Rev. Abiel Abbot noted this transformation as early as 1818 in, of all Charlestonians, the daughters of David and Martha Laurens Ramsay. He wrote of a conversation that he had had with them: "It was soon evident from what pedigree their minds sprang & under whose fostering tuition they had risen from infancy to adult years. There was a very remarkable precision of thought & expression & manner in every one of the ladies, what they said was in measured periods fit to be in type. It could not fail to be incident to manner of conversation like this that a degree of formality would at times be apparent, inspiring a caution a little chilling on the flow of mind & soul. It is easily accounted for. They are continually under the impression that they are regarded as the models of the young ladies in their school—& that nothing must appear in the example but precise perfection. To this manner also the consciousness that they are the off-spring of illustrious ancestors & parents whose names are embalmed in the national history & their lives & writings & piety preserved among the choicest treasures of American biography doubtless contributes not a little."

This search for the past was conscious. It is apparent in the great amount of name changing. William Smith, in 1804, added Loughton as his middle name; Joseph Allen Smith assumed Izard as his last name. John Lynch Bowman changed his name to John Bowman Lynch. Francis Marion provided in his will that his nephew must assume the name of Francis Marion in order to inherit his estate. The practice became so common that in 1814 the state passed a law making it easier to change the name of a family. The most famous use of this law was made in 1837 when the six Smith brothers of Beaufort asked to change their names from Smith to Rhett so that, as the petitioners said, "the name of Rhett, in the grandmaternal line, and now extinct, may be revived and . . . consecrated by natural regard and affection." Robert Barnwell Rhett, the father of secession, was the prime example.

In such a society, where thoughts were freezing into a permanent form, what was the place of education? Thomas Smith Grimké, almost alone among his contemporaries, expounded a theory of education which would act as a bridge to the future. In a speech in Charleston in 1827 and in another at Yale in 1830 before the Phi Beta Kappa Society, he attacked education "on the Catholic principle" that students "must read with a submissive faith, that they must believe *all* in Homer and Vergil, in Horace and Theocritus to be poetry—*all* in Cicero and Demosthenes to be eloquence—*all* in Thucydides and Herodotus, in Livy and Tacitus, to be unrivalled in History." He attacked rote memorization of the classics. He wanted education to be based "on the Protestant principle" that one must "think and reason" for oneself. Grimké, like David Ramsay before him, saw in the ideals of the Protestant Reformation and the American Revolution fertilizing currents. The drift of his thinking was that human learning should be used to enlighten people and to meliorate the condition of man. He hoped that America (for his thoughts were never provincial) would become "a republic of thought."

Hugh Swinton Legaré took up Grimké's challenge in the first article in the *Southern Review* and defended classical learning against modern or scientific learning. According to Legaré, one should study in order to observe beauty, not to improve the condition of mankind. One should study the beauty that is eternal in nature. The beauty is always there; it is the same for all, no matter what a man's place in the ranks of society. Legaré revealed these ideas best in his review of Jeremy Bentham's work. For Legaré, natural instincts were unchanging, and law should be built on this premise. Above all, he challenged Bentham's idea that positive legislation could produce the greatest happiness of the greatest number.

Both Grimké and Legaré were aware of the decline of Charleston. Grimké thought of a new system of education as a way out. Legaré turned to European examples of decline for an understanding of the problem. Could an examination of the causes of the decline of Venice provide a lesson for Charleston? Legaré came to these thoughts after reading James Fenimore Cooper's European romance, *The Bravo*. This novel, he stated in the *Southern Review*, was designed to exhibit "the moral emanating from the social operations of the Venetian system": "Thus when we read in the novel under review, and in other modern works, saddening relations of the prostrate and torpid conditions of Venice, certain resemblances in her situation and history, with those of this once flourishing city, bring them home to us with a sharp adaptation. Having their origin in common from religious intolerance and persecution, the colonists who took refuge at Grado, and amidst the Lagunes of Venice, and the Huguenots who fled to these shores, have other points of assimilation in the site, fortunes and look of the cities they respectively founded. Beneath a southerly clime and sunny skies, in a champain country, and with a choice harbour, the structures of their sanctuaries, as you approach from the water of Sullivan's Island, corresponding to the Lido, forcibly induce a mutual recollection—and when the moon has thrown its light around, as the solitary passenger, through the deserted and sepulchral streets of Charleston, meditates upon her time-worn, rusty, and mouldering edifices, he is gloomily reminded of the blank, icy, and desolate aspect of that other city afar; now manifestly 'expiring before the eyes' of her inhabitants, and fast 'sinking into the slime of her own canals.' " Perhaps there was something seductive in the charm of decay.

In this society the inquiring mind turned to the natural sciences. The Rev. John Bachman, born in 1790, was the principal figure in the local circle of natural scientists. He had written monographs on squirrels and rabbits. He was the friend of Audubon, the great ornithologist, who had made his way to Charleston in the 1820's, and the two had collaborated in the writing of *The Viviparous Quadrupeds of North America*, which appeared in three volumes between 1845 and 1849. A relative of the Pinckneys by marriage, John Edward Holbrook, a zoologist, specializing in the study of reptiles and fish, had published a five-volume *North American Herpetology* in 1842. In 1855 he printed his *Ichthyology of South Carolina*. Edmund Ravenel, a South Carolina planter, had become interested in shells while staying at his summer home on Sullivan's Island. He was the pioneer American naturalist in the field of conchology and produced a work on sea urchins in 1848. He was the model for William Legrand in Poe's "The Gold Bug," a Huguenot of decayed fortunes, a seeker of shells. Henry William Ravenel, a botanist interested in fungi, mosses, and lichens, published his findings between 1855 and 1860 in five volumes. St. Julien Ravenel, the nephew of Edmund, was to use his knowledge of agricultural chemistry after the war to develop fertilizer from the phosphate deposits of the state. Francis Peyre Porcher combined interests in medicine and botany and issued in 1849 *A Sketch of the Medical Botany of South Carolina*.

This group of scientists was interested in the gathering of facts from the world around them. They shared their interest with the professors of the College of Charleston and of the new South Carolina Medical College. But it was an investigation locked in frameworks of the past. It has often been said that Darwin's theories were expounded in Charleston by Langdon Cheves before the publication of the *Origin of the Species* in 1859. But it should be noted that these men did not carry over their new insights from the world of plants and animals to the world of men. To have done so would have brought them face to face with change in human society, a fact they did not wish to face. They were not social scientists. They did on one occasion spend an evening at Christopher Gustavus Memminger's discussing the "social systems most conducive to human happiness." The answer they obviously reached was that their own was such. In 1850, Bachman published *The Doctrine of the Unity of the Human Race*, in which he admitted the unity of humankind but devoted most of his efforts to an attempt to reconcile science with the Scriptures. William James Rivers, Charleston's historian and a member of the Memminger circle, phrased this dilemma in a poem written on the occasion of Bachman's death:

Though with her treasures Science wooed thy mind,
And nature brought, as to her votary, flowers
And fruits, and from each distant region, bird
And beast, as erst in Eden, to be named—
Still ever to the Father's will revealed,
Pure fountain of His truth, thy thought was turned,
And ever, with unquestioning trust, was heard
His mandate to go forth and preach His Word,
That haply it might kindle in our souls
The faith and love and hope that quickened thine.

In the realm of the arts, by the 1830's Charlestonians had turned away from cosmopolitanism to a conservative sectional patriotism. At the end of the eighteenth century and at the beginning of the nineteenth, those who went abroad brought back art: old masters, eighteenth-century views in the manner of Canaletto, and contemporary portraits by West and Copley. In 1791 an art exhibition raised funds for the new College of Charleston. William Loughton Smith, returning in 1804 with many treasures, put them on display for his friends in the new home of Gabriel Manigault. In 1816 there was a loan exhibition of paintings in the South Carolina Society Hall to start a new institution, but it was not until 1821 that the South Carolina Academy of Fine Arts was incorporated and not until 1823 that it held its first exhibition. Samuel F. B. Morse, John Stevens Cogdell (the friend of Washington Allston), John Blake White, Joel Roberts Poinsett, and Charles Fraser were the men behind this organization. But there was little support for it. When Henry Ravenel objected to having the Academy built close to his own home, the city council sustained his objections and ordered the Academy to be built elsewhere. The Academy joined in a lottery with the Literary and Philosophical Society, but it did not raise much money. Cogdell, himself a devoted patron of the arts, could not win the state as a patron of the Academy. On July 22, 1830, the institution closed. Many of the finer things died in the nullification crisis, among them the *South Carolina Law Quarterly Journal* and the *Southern Review*. John Vanderlyn wrote in 1835 that the "real sufferers" from the "angry feelings" aroused by nullification were men like himself—the artists. When the Carolina Art Association was formed in 1858, the first exhibition was built around Emanuel Leutze's "Jasper Rescuing the Flag at Fort Moultrie." For Charlestonians, art was merely visual history.

There was a group of men in Charleston who tried to grapple with the economic decline. Most of them were members of the commercial community, men who had been arriving from the North and in a few instances still from England, the group that had fertilized the commercial and intellectual life of the community since the 1730's. In 1819 they could be found among the membership of the newly organized New England Society. Most importantly, they were the ones who between 1828 and 1832 succeeded in building a railroad to Hamburg on the Savannah River in an effort to tap the trade of the new Southwest, the trade that was beginning to find an outlet through Mobile and New Orleans. William Aiken raised the funds; Robert Eason and Thomas Dotterer tried to build the engines; and the Lucases, that enterprising family from England, tried to build the steamships to carry what was brought to the port to England. The steamships floundered; the railroad efforts never solved the local economic problems. What was lacking was business acumen in the new industrial age. When the Duke of Saxe-Weimar visited Lucas' rice mill on the Ashley in 1826 and learned that a new steam machine of twenty-four horsepower would be brought out from England, he commented: "It is wonderful, however, that the best steam-engines must be made in England to supply a country that has numbered ROBERT FULTON among her citizens!" The attitude of the city is best expressed in the fact that, as the building of the railroad drew near the city, the city would not let the company lay tracks to the wharves. The railroad must stop at Line Street, the 1814 line of fortifications and the city limits of those days. All freight must be transshipped to wagons and hauled to the docks. The advantage of bypassing Savannah was thus lost in the city of Charleston herself. And so Charleston held up her hand to the smoking engines and said, "Do not enter."

Nullification was the hand against the nation. An elite knows no better way of protecting itself than by playing the role of protector of older and higher orders, or predecessors, or the Constitution, or justice, or the law, or God Himself. It was a sign of the weakness of this group that it must now hide behind the Constitution. It was John C. Calhoun who forged the constitutional doctrine of nullification, which had as its prime purpose to cut all national ties established in 1787. Power to collect the tariff in Charleston would be denied. Power to appeal from decisions of state courts into federal courts would be denied. Oaths of allegiance to the state would be required.

The crucial battle in 1832 and 1833 in Charleston was not so much tariff or no tariff, or slavery or no slavery, as it was whether or not the city should be of the world. The battle was as bitter as any in the history of the city. In September, 1832, each side locked up opponents so that they could not vote. The two parties almost rioted when a man fell out of a fourth-floor window of a house in Queen Street, which was then occupied by the Union party. Jacob Schirmer commented in his diary: "The most disgraceful acts resorted to by both parties sufficient to cause the most awful visitations from a just and offended God." Two years later, when the test oath divided parties, Schirmer again commented in his diary: "The manner in which it was conducted was too disgraceful to record for any future generation to read. It was awful to the extreme." With passions at such a height, the losers could expect no mercy. And they got none. The leaders of the Unionists, many of whom were old Federalists, were driven from public life. William Drayton moved to Philadelphia. Joel R. Poinsett, after being rewarded with the position of secretary of war by Martin Van Buren, came home to a life of obscurity. Having married a rich widow, he retired to the banks of the Black River, where, in 1850, Fredrika Bremer found him living almost as if in exile.

The campaign to mold one monolithic society was relentless. For men in public office who had taken an oath to uphold the United States Constitution, the state oath, as it was then phrased, posed a cruel dilemma. The purpose was to force each man to make a personal choice for the state or against it. When the abolitionists began to flood the mails with literature, Alfred Huger, the Charleston postmaster, sorted out the objectionable material and did not deliver it. When there was a protest against this interference with the federal mails, the local mob, led by respectable citizens, destroyed the pamphlets before they could be delivered. When Postmaster-General Amos Kendall was consulted in Washington, he condoned the nondelivery of this type of mail. It was also in 1835 that the state legislature passed a law stating that slaves should not be taught to read or to write. They might be expounded to orally only by white men. When Congress itself became deluged with petitions on the subject of slavery, the Charleston representative in Congress, Henry Laurens Pinckney, urged that body to adopt a gag rule which would prevent discussion of that subject. And so the campaign to silence criticism went on.

Although the city lost population in this decade, outwardly the city was as grand as ever. When fire destroyed St. Philip's church in 1835, it was rebuilt as handsomely as ever. The great fire of April 27 and 28, 1838, covered a larger area than any previous fire. It started near the corner of Market and King and, fanned by a southwest wind, burned through to the Cooper River, just missing the Pinckney mansion on the south and the Laurens mansion on the north. King Street, the retail center of trade lined with wooden buildings, suffered a total loss on both sides of the street from Market to Liberty. The loss in the city was four million dollars. Yet the homes that were built after 1838

163

in this burned-over area were so handsomely designed and solidly built that they are being restored today by Historic Charleston's Ansonborough project.

Many fine homes were built in other parts of town during the 1840's and 1850's: the Mikell home on Montagu and Rutledge, the Faber villa on East Bay, and the Alston, Ravenel, and DeSaussure homes on High Battery behind the new sea wall. But these homes lacked something in taste; they were less refined than their earlier neighbors. One need only compare Patrick O'Donnell's house on King with its neighbor to the north, the Miles Brewton house.

Charlestonians, by the eve of the Civil War, believed that they had the perfect society. In the 1830's in Europe and in the North, there was a search for utopias. While the Saint Simonians and the Fourierists were dividing men into functions that they performed according to their capacities and Marx was dividing them into classes, the Charlestonians knew that they had the answer in the division by race. While the North sought solutions at New Harmony or in the Oneida Community or at Brook Farm, the Charlestonians listened to Calhoun and believed. When Calhoun said in 1837 that slavery was a good, they understood. This was why there was such great pressure upon the free Negro in the local society, for it was now thought that the best division of society would be into free white men and slave black men. They were divided also into functions. Some would work, and some would cultivate the arts. Even Joel Roberts Poinsett, speaking in 1834 on the "Natural Progress of the Human Race," had to confess that the main reason for the immutable condition of mankind was the "invincible repugnance of mankind, to submit to the restraints imposed by the labour of agricultural pursuits. . . ."

The conclusion was that one race should labor and one should cultivate civilization. The idea of a Greek democracy became utterly appealing.

Charleston thus became the center of an idea, a southern way of life. And from this center these ideas began to penetrate throughout the nation. William Grayson's "The Hireling and the Slave" was its greatest statement, but J. G. B. DeBow, who had moved from Charleston to New Orleans, was its greatest propagandist. But when men like Chief Justice Roger B. Taney and Senator Stephen A. Douglas seemed to take up these views, Abraham Lincoln saw that they must be opposed. When Charleston became the place of meeting for the Democratic party in 1860, it was quite simply a contest between Lincoln and Charleston. It was altogether fitting that the war should begin at Fort Sumter in Charleston harbor.

So appealing had these ideas become by 1861 that Charleston believed that God was on her side. At least her clergy told her so. The Rev. Thomas Smyth, in his discourse preached on June 13, 1861, the day of thanksgiving for the glorious victory at Fort Sumter, spoke of that victory as "a signal proof of the powerful providence of God; and, secondly, as a pledge and promise of God's continued providence and protection over us." The supreme statement of this message was made in the Rev. James Warley Miles' sermon, entitled, "God in History," which was delivered before the graduating class of the College of Charleston in March, 1863. "No people have existed wholly without a meaning." Charleston had a mission to act for the blessing or the curse of humanity. ". . . the stream of humanity has always manifested its capacity for the development of higher civilization as it flowed westward from its

Asiatic home—thus indicating a gradual unfolding of the divine plan or idea of man." The Rev. James Warley Miles concluded: "we have the glorious, but awfully responsible mission of exhibiting to the world that supremest effort of humanity—the foundation of a political organization, in which the freedom of every member is the result of law, is preserved by justice, is harmonized by the true relations of labor and capital, and is sanctioned by the divine spirit of Christianity."

Epilogue

On April 25 and 26, 1850, Charleston, having dressed herself in mourning, paid homage to John C. Calhoun. On the morning of the twenty-fifth, Calhoun's funeral cortege assembled on Marion Square in front of The Citadel. It moved out into Boundary Street (soon to be renamed Calhoun Street) through gates supported by palmettos draped in mourning. The cavalry, the federal and state troops, and the mayor and aldermen of the city preceded the magnificent hearse, which itself was flanked by a guard of honor and the distinguished pallbearers, among whom was Jefferson Davis. Then came the family, the Congressional delegation, the Governor, the state officials, the representatives of the colleges and the schools, the societies, the fraternal orders, the captains of vessels, the seamen, all interspersed with bands. This procession marched down King Street to Hasell, through Hasell to Meeting, down Meeting to South Bay and the Battery, along the Battery to East Bay, and then up East Bay to Broad Street and to the City Hall. There the coffin was placed on a magnificent catafalque, past which the townspeople filed during the ensuing twenty-four hours while an honor guard of two hundred citizens kept the vigil. On the next day the procession reassembled and accompanied the body to St. Philip's Church, where, after a brief but moving ceremony, the body was laid to rest in the western cemetery of the church. London, paying her honors to the Duke of Wellington, could not have done more.

It was ironic that Charleston should pay such homage to

Calhoun. He had said in 1807 that the fever in Charleston was "a curse for their intemperance and debaucheries." But this upcountry man had become the defender of the city's way of life. As Pitt had been the hero on the eve of the Revolution, so Calhoun became the hero on the eve of the Civil War. It was appropriate that the citizens, just as they had once erected a monument to Pitt and placed it at the center of the city, should now erect a tall monument to Calhoun and place it in Marion Square, overlooking the city that did him so much honor.

But Calhoun's legacy, the ultimate defense of secession, was not enough. The war came, and the city was destroyed. It was as if God and the Yankees were venting their wrath. On December 11, 1861, a great fire, starting on the Cooper River and driven by a northeast wind of almost hurricane force, swept through the heart of the town, doing five to seven million dollars' worth of damage before it expired on the banks of the Ashley. The flames rushed through, "almost like forked lightning . . . red hot tiles and slates falling and striking [citizens] upon the head and shoulders as they worked to halt the fire. Five churches were destroyed: the Circular [Congregational Church], the Cumberland St. Methodist, St. Peter's Episcopal on Logan St., the Quaker Meeting on King, and the new Catholic cathedral of St. John's and St. Finbar's." The spire of St. John's and St. Finbar's "fell with a terrific crash, sounding high above the noise of the devouring flames." St. Andrew's Hall and Institute Hall, both associated with secession decrees, were consumed. Finally, "the fine old mansion of the Pinckney family, on East Bay, [fell] a prey to the devouring element. . . ." Later, during the longest siege in modern times, there rained in on the city from Morris Island bombs tossed by the Swamp Angel, a gun whose shells reached as far north as Calhoun Street. Finally, on the day of the surrender of the city, February 17, 1865, the ammunition dump blew up with a great explosion. Charleston lay in ruins.

Late in that spring of 1865, Caroline Gilman, the wife of the Unitarian minister Samuel Gilman, who had died in 1858, made her way back to Charleston from Greenville where she had taken refuge. Along the way she saw, as she confided to her diary, "scarcely a farm house, not an elegant and hospitable plantation residence on the way, all ruin, ruin; and in Columbia the last rays of twilight were on the ruins." She added: "In 1858 I journeyed with a coffin, where was laid my love and earthly hope, and came home. In 1865 I journeyed with the dead South, and came home." What she saw was a city devastated, her home plundered of all books, private papers, pictures, her church's cemetery filled with the debris and overgrowth of four years of war and neglect. Yet many flowers bloomed amid the ruins. And so she sighed: "I could not help thinking yesterday, as I saw the flowers look up and smile when the superincumbent weight and decay and ruin were removed, that they set us a good example politically. But then, flowers have no memory."

Bibliographical Note

THIS BOOK is based primarily on original research. Out of research that I have done over the past ten years both at home and abroad have come three volumes besides this one: George C. Rogers, Jr., *Evolution of a Federalist: William Loughton Smith of Charleston (1758–1812)* (Columbia, S.C., 1962); *The Papers of Henry Laurens*, I, ed. Philip M. Hamer and George C. Rogers, Jr. (Columbia, S.C., 1968); and George C. Rogers, Jr., *The History of Georgetown County, South Carolina* (Columbia, S.C., 1970). Information and ideas have also been drawn from the sources listed below.

CHAPTER I: Edward McCrady, *The History of South Carolina under the Royal Government, 1719–1776* (New York, 1899); Robert L. Meriwether, *The Expansion of South Carolina, 1729–1765* (Kingsport, Tenn., 1940); Leila Sellers, *Charleston Business on the Eve of the American Revolution* (Chapel Hill, N.C., 1934); William Simpson, *The Practical Justice of the Peace and Parish-Officer of His Majesty's Province of South Carolina* (Charlestown, S.C., 1761).

CHAPTER II: Joseph I. Waring, *A History of Medicine in South Carolina, 1670–1825* (Columbia, S.C., 1964); David M. Ludlum, *Early American Hurricanes, 1492–1870* (Boston, 1963); M. Eugene Sirmans, *Colonial South Carolina, A Political History, 1663–1763* (Chapel Hill, N.C., 1966); Jack P. Greene, *The Quest for Power, The Lower Houses of Assembly in the Southern Royal Colonies, 1689–1776* (Chapel Hill, N.C., 1963); Richard Maxwell Brown,

The South Carolina Regulators (Cambridge, Mass., 1963); Edward McCrady, *The History of South Carolina in the Revolution, 1775–1780* (New York, 1901); Edward Mc-Crady, *The History of South Carolina in the Revolution, 1780–1783* (New York, 1902); William Moultrie, *Memoirs of the American Revolution* (2 vols., New York, 1802).

CHAPTER III: Samuel Gaillard Stoney, *This is Charleston, A Survey of the Architectural Heritage of a Unique American City* (Charleston, S.C., 1964); Beatrice St. Julien Ravenel, *Architects of Charleston* (Charleston, S.C., 1945); Alston Deas, *The Early Ironwork of Charleston* (Columbia, S.C., 1941); A. R. H. Smith and D. E. H. Smith, *The Dwelling Houses of Charleston, South Carolina* (Philadelphia, 1917); "Journal of Josiah Quincy, Junior, 1773," *Proceedings of the Massachusetts Historical Society*, Vol. XLIX (1915–16), 443–50; E. Milby Burton, *Charleston Furniture, 1700–1825* (Charleston, S.C., 1955); E. Milby Burton, *South Carolina Silversmiths, 1690–1860* (Charleston, S.C., 1942); Anna Wells Rutledge, "Artists in the Life of Charleston," *Transactions of the American Philosophical Society*, Vol. XXXIX, Part 2 (1939); Lorenzo Dow Turner, *Africanisms in the Gullah Dialect* (Chicago, 1949); John Bennett, "Gullah: A Negro Patois," *South Atlantic Quarterly*, Vol. VIII (January, 1909), 39–52; Sarah Rutledge, *The Carolina Housewife* (Charleston, S.C., 1847); Beatrice St. Julien Ravenel, *Charleston, The Place and the People* (New York, 1929).

CHAPTER IV: Frederick P. Bowes, *The Culture of Early Charleston* (Chapel Hill, N.C., 1942); Frederick Dalcho, *An Historical Account of the Protestant Episcopal Church in South Carolina . . .* (Charleston, S.C., 1820); Alexander

Hewat, *A Historical Account of the Rise and Progress of the Colonies of South Carolina and Georgia* (2 vols., London, 1779); David Ramsay, *The History of the Independent or Congregational Church in Charleston, South Carolina, from its Origin till the Year 1814* (Philadelphia, 1815); Brooke Hindle, *The Pursuit of Science in Revolutionary America, 1735–1789* (Chapel Hill, N.C., 1956); Carl Bridenbaugh, *Myths and Realities, Societies of the Colonial South* (Baton Rouge, La., 1952); Carl Bridenbaugh, *Cities in Revolt, Urban Life in America, 1743–1776* (New York, 1964); Caroline Robbins, *The Eighteenth-Century Commonwealthman* (Cambridge, Mass., 1961); J. G. A. Pocock, "Machiavelli, Harrington, and English Political Ideologies in the Eighteenth Century," *William and Mary Quarterly*, Vol. XXII (October, 1965), 549–83; Edmund S. Morgan, "The Puritan Ethic and the American Revolution," *William and Mary Quarterly*, Vol. XXIV (January, 1967), 3–43; "David Ramsay, 1749–1815, Selections from his Writings," ed. Robert L. Brunhouse, *Transactions of the American Philosophical Society*, Vol. LV (1965); Eola Willis, *The Charleston Stage in the XVIII Century* (Columbia, S.C., 1924); John B. Irving, *The South Carolina Jockey Club* (Charleston, S.C., 1857).

CHAPTER V: Marvin R. Zahniser, *Charles Cotesworth Pinckney, Founding Father* (Chapel Hill, N.C., 1967); David H. Fischer, *The Revolution of American Conservatism, The Federalist Party in the Era of Jeffersonian Democracy* (New York, 1965); Alfred G. Smith, Jr., *Economic Readjustment of an Old Cotton State, South Carolina, 1820–1860* (Columbia, S.C., 1958).

CHAPTER VI: John Lofton, *Insurrection in South Carolina: The Turbulent World of Denmark Vesey* (Yellow

Springs, Ohio, 1964); Donald G. Morgan, *Justice William Johnson, the First Dissenter* (Columbia, S.C., 1954); *Southern Review*, Vols. I–VIII (1828–32); Alexander Garden, *Anecdotes of the Revolutionary War in America, with Sketches of Character of Persons the Most Distinguished, in the Southern States, for Civil and Military Services* (Charleston, S.C., 1822); William Johnson, *Sketches of the Life and Correspondence of Nathanael Greene* ...(2 vols., Charleston, S.C., 1822); "The Abiel Abbot Journals, A Yankee Preacher in Charleston Society, 1818–27," ed. John Hammond Moore, *South Carolina Historical Magazine*, Vol. LXVIII (1967), 51–73, 115–39, 232–54; Bernhard, Duke of Saxe-Weimar Eisenach, *Travels through North America during the Years 1825 and 1826* (2 vols., Philadelphia, 1828); Samuel M. Derrick, *Centennial History of South Carolina Railroad* (Columbia, S.C., 1930); William W. Freehling, *Prelude to Civil War, the Nullification Controversy in South Carolina, 1816–1836* (New York, 1965).

Index